GIFT OF THE
CLAYTON COMMUNITY
LIBRARY FOUNDATION

WITHDRAWN

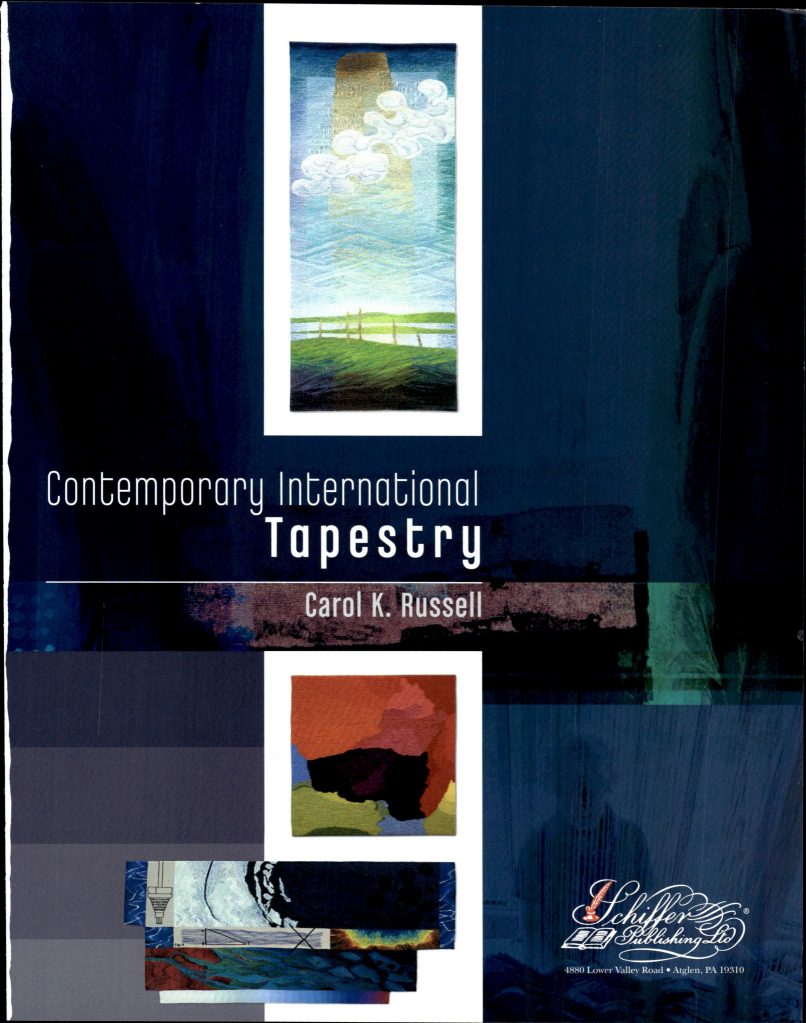

Contemporary International Tapestry

Carol K. Russell

Schiffer Publishing Ltd
4880 Lower Valley Road • Atglen, PA 19310

Other Schiffer Books by the Author:
Tapestry Handbook: The Next Generation, $59.95
ISBN: 978-0-7643-2756-8
Fiber Art Today, $50.00
ISBN: 978-0-7643-3777-2

Copyright © 2015 by Carol K. Russell

Library of Congress Control Number: 201495019

All rights reserved. No part of this work may be reproduced or used in any form or by any means—graphic, electronic, or mechanical, including photocopying or information storage and retrieval systems—without written permission from the publisher.

The scanning, uploading, and distribution of this book or any part thereof via the Internet or via any other means without the permission of the publisher is illegal and punishable by law. Please purchase only authorized editions and do not participate in or encourage the electronic piracy of copyrighted materials.
"Schiffer," "Schiffer Publishing, Ltd. & Design," and the "Design of pen and inkwell" are registered trademarks of Schiffer Publishing, Ltd.

Designed by Justin Watkinson
Cover by Danielle Farmer
Type set in ChaletComprime/Minion Pro

ISBN: 978-0-7643-4869-3
Printed in China

Published by Schiffer Publishing, Ltd.
4880 Lower Valley Road
Atglen, PA 19310
Phone: (610) 593-1777; Fax: (610) 593-2002
E-mail: Info@schifferbooks.com

For our complete selection of fine books on this and related subjects, please visit our website at www.schifferbooks.com.
You may also write for a free catalog.

This book may be purchased from the publisher.
Please try your bookstore first.

We are always looking for people to write books on new and related subjects. If you have an idea for a book, please contact us at proposals@schifferbooks.com.

Schiffer Publishing's titles are available at special discounts for bulk purchases for sales promotions or premiums. Special editions, including personalized covers, corporate imprints, and excerpts can be created in large quantities for special needs.
For more information, contact the publisher.

Acknowledgment

The Hunterdon Art Museum, a center for art, craft, and design, is proud to present the exhibition *Contemporary International Tapestry*, which brings together work by approximately forty artists from North America, Asia, and Europe. The exhibition's curator, Carol K. Russell, one of the leading experts in the field of tapestry, has selected important work by major international artists, providing an unusual opportunity to see under one roof current trends in contemporary tapestry. A curated exhibition of new work on this scale has not been seen in the Northeast for many years.

On behalf of the Museum's board of trustees, I wish to thank Carol K. Russell for her extraordinary dedication to this project. Carol has organized an exhibition of beautiful objects made by practitioners who employ the highest standards and exceptional techniques. Writing about those artists in this publication, Carol has given both the casual observer of tapestry and the aficionado an informative and delightful book that will be of interest to those who view the exhibition as well as those who wish to learn about the subject for years to come.

We are fortunate to have essays by Archie Brennan, Christine Laffer, and Lycia Trouton in this publication. Their intimate relationships with artists, galleries, museums, and our unique international community give a perspective that is insightful and rare. We thank them for being a part of *Contemporary International Tapestry*.

Our gratitude goes to The Coby Foundation, Ltd. and, in particular, its Executive Director Ward L. E. Mintz for the Foundation's generous support of this exhibition. The Coby Foundation's interest in textiles makes it a unique and important partner in an exhibition devoted to tapestry. We also wish to thank the New Jersey State Council on the Arts and the Geraldine R. Dodge Foundation for their general operating support. Additionally, we are grateful to Nancy Schiffer of Schiffer Publishing, Ltd. for her special appreciation of tapestry and all the textile arts.

We thank the lenders to this exhibition whose generosity has made this show possible. Sincere appreciation goes to Caroline and Roger Ford; Temple Emanu-El of Westfield, New Jersey; and collectors who wish to remain anonymous.

Special thanks go to Rick Snyderman of Snyderman Works Gallery, Philadelphia. We are grateful for his assistance in locating and obtaining certain tapestries as well as for his generosity of spirit.

With great respect and admiration, we thank the artists included in this exhibition. They are at the forefront of the field—artists who have made important contributions by advancing techniques, employing inventive materials, and creating tapestries that are a significant part of contemporary art.

Last, but certainly not least, thanks also are extended to the Hunterdon Art Museum's staff and volunteers for their work on *Contemporary International Tapestry*. In particular we thank Rosemary Maravetz, the Museum's Exhibitions Coordinator, for her diligence and invaluable service to this project, and Ingrid Renard and Ellen Siegel of our installation crew for their expertise and dedication in installing this show.

Marjorie Frankel Nathanson
Executive Director
Hunterdon Art Museum
7 Lower Center Street
Clinton, New Jersey 08809-1303
Tel. 908-735-8415
http://hunterdonartmuseum.org

Blue Dog Motel

♣ Old Highway 13 ♣
Truck Parking, Kitchenettes
Music every Friday

Once upon a forest in a deep dark
time there lived a woman who made
things and a man who broke them.
The woman made ~~love~~ beds
and bread and tea.
She made shirts and
excuses. She made do.
The man broke horses and
ground and crockery. He
broke tools and bones and
promises. She thought he had
broken her spirit. But one
morning she made up her
mind. And broke away.

Sarah C. Swett. *Rough Copy 1: Blue Dog Motel.* Handwoven tapestry: wool warp and weft, natural dye. 45 x 35" (112.5 x 87.5cm).
Photo: Mark LaMoreaux.

The Sketchbook

The sketchbook was new, its pages thick and blank. The yarn was asparagus green. "Braised asparagus," murmured the woman as she tucked the skein beside the book, "with a glimmer of parsley. Lovely."

Not so the ink in the squat glass jar she packed next which had the hue and character of horse piss. But she gave it a swish just the same and nestled it into the saddlebag, safe among strands of wool. Piss or asparagus, it was ink she had made—and the only ink for more miles than she cared to contemplate—so she was damned if she'd put it at risk. Running off with the mule was reckless enough.

The mule was unhinged. Or so some people said. The woman preferred 'mercurial' and 'moonstruck', but semantics aside she couldn't deny that what the animal did best was break things—or that a bit of caution with a glass jar was prudent. And it pleased her to be prudent about something since her selection of spur-of-the-moment supplies left so much to be desired.

"We'll list our regrets when we've gone," she whispered to the mule. And knotting yesterday's braids at the nape of her neck, she tightened the cinch, swung her thigh over the saddle, and slipped into the hills.

Sarah C. Swett. *Rough Copy 2: The Sketchbook*. Handwoven tapestry: wool warp and weft, natural dye. 70 x 36" (175 x 90cm). Photo: Mark LaMoreaux.

Contents

An Artist's Life in Tapestry..........9
By Archie Brennan OBE

Exhibiting Changes...............11
by Christine Laffer

Embedded Narratives:
A Canadian perspective on tapestry
as a permeable and public art.....14
by Lycia Trouton PhD

Contemporary International Tapestry . 17
Introduction by Carol K. Russell

The Artists.... 22

- Jo Barker 23
- Joan Baxter 24
- Helga Berry.............. 26
- Rebecca Bluestone 28
- Archie Brennan 30
- Elizabeth J. Buckley 31
- Soyoo Park Caltabiano 32
- Włodzimierz Cygan 38
- Alla Davydova 41
- Lise DeCoursin............ 43
- Susan T. Edmunds 44
- Alexandra Schilling Friedman . 45
- Ina Golub 46
- Barbara Heller 48
- Susan Hart Henegar........ 51
- Silvia Heyden............. 52
- Dirk Holger 53
- Peter Horn 54
- Constance Hunt 56
- Susan Iverson 58
- Ruth Jones 59
- Aino Kajaniemi............ 60
- Jane Kidd................. 61
- Lialia Kuchma 64
- Christine Laffer 65
- Ewa Latkowska-Żychska.... 66
- Bojana H. Leznicki 68
- Lore Kadden Lindenfeld 69
- Yael Lurie & Jean Pierre Larochette............. 70
- Luis Lazo 71
- Susan Martin Maffei 72
- Julia Mitchell............. 74
- Janet Moore.............. 76
- Jon Eric Riis.............. 80
- Ramona Sakiestewa 82
- Micala Sidore 83
- Elinor Steele 85
- Sarah Swett.............. 86
- Linda Wallace............. 88

Glossary 91

Bibliography .. 96

Appendix 102

- Artists' Websites 102
- Galleries and Dealers 103
- Museums and Collections... 105
- Exhibitions............... 108
- Periodicals............... 109
- Professional Organizations ..110
- Art Textiles Conservation and Restoration 111

398.233
Sw47f

Swett, Sarah C.
A Field Guide
to Needlework

DATE	ISSUED TO
19 Aug	W. Edwards
28 Dec	Lois Bladden
13 Jan	Gabrielle Swit

Neither she nor the mule had wandered much beyond berry-gathering distance from home, but they chose an overgrown path — the third on the left — and embroidered themselves into the forest as though they knew what they were about

DEMCO 32-208

Sarah C. Swett. *Rough Copy 3: A Field Guide.* Handwoven tapestry: wool warp and weft,

An Artist's Life in Tapestry

by Archie Brennan OBE

In 1947 I began my seven-year-long, full-time apprenticeship in woven tapestry at Dovecot Studios in Edinburgh, Scotland. It happened by chance. As a 16-year-old, I was still in high school, and wished to find a career in the visual arts. I heard that I could attend evening classes at Edinburgh's College of Art, drawing from a live model four times a week. There I met two apprentices in tapestry who invited me to visit Dovecot Studios. Ironically the workshop was only some 300 yards north of my family home. Although I knew of the ancient stone dovecote, I had no awareness of the tapestry studios built there in 1911. Anyway, they asked me to bring along some of my own drawings and artworks, and subsequently invited me to start an apprenticeship.

That was 67 years ago. I still weave tapestry every day. I undertook graduate and post-graduate studies at the college in tapestry, stained glass, drawing, and painting. I was then invited to set up a department of woven tapestry. It grew and grew, with students applying from many countries. Curiously, 90 percent were female at a time when the Dovecot staff, as with French workshops, comprised only male weavers.

I mention that story because today the American Tapestry Alliance (ATA) is 95 percent female, with some 900 memberships. From medieval times until the 1940s in France, Netherlands, and Italy, tapestry weaving was strictly men's work. Women were permitted only to spin and wind yarns. Interestingly, in convents in Switzerland and Germany, the nuns were tapestry weavers. Although I admire so many early medieval mural-size tapestries, I take special delight in those many tapestries from the convents. It is significant also that so-called Coptic, Peruvian, Norwegian, Swedish, and Danish tapestries of special quality were woven in homes by women.

However, major changes in the approach to tapestries were occurring in southwestern Europe during this time, with a focus on large mural tapestries by the male weavers. They were usually "landscape" in shape. Designs were painted by nonweaving painters, as were full-size working drawings (cartoons). The tapestry cloth became much finer with the warp set at 18, even up to 40-plus warp ends per inch, and a "hatching" technique developed to handle the light-to-dark imagery of the designs, with many weft-filled bobbins hanging in front and waiting to be used over the woven surface. The weavers shifted to the back of the loom, using mirrors at the front. This approach is still popular in many tapestry workshops, as it was at Dovecot Studios.

I had spent some time as an itinerant weaver in France with a small, portable upright loom. I was intent on exploring discreet surface changes using a variety of weft yarns—cotton, linen, even tapestry warp, and I moved to the front of the loom to examine the result in a strong cross-light. By the late 1950s, I had switched all the techniques of my training and never again wove from behind the loom.

An interesting event occurred at the Dovecot some years later. I had been appointed head weaver, and we had been commissioned to weave a 7-foot-high by 14-foot-long tapestry for a new government building with a fixed opening date. For technical reasons we were weaving from the side: four weavers at a 7-foot-wide warp. I wove from the front and the others wove from the back in their usual way. They were crowded, so Fred offered to try weaving from the front. He loved it. Before long, Douglas asked to move to the front. He loved it, so I moved to the back, until Harry asked to move to the front. We met the deadline, but I spent long nights at the loom alone. That was 50 years ago, and since then the entire staff weaves from the front, a team that includes both male and female. Maureen Hodge and Fiona Matheson joined the staff after graduating from college in Edinburgh and London.

Before all this, Dovecot had faltered. A new government tax system had reduced the number of projects. Ron Cruickshank, then head weaver, decided to set up his own studio and invited me to join him. I did, and finished my final two years of apprenticeship with him. Together we wove a good number of tapestries by British and French artists who had already designed tapestries in Europe. Then my military service was due. Ron moved to Baton Rouge, La., and I moved to France and began the exploration I described earlier.

Why was the general approach to tapestry-making so reproductive, with a prepared design, rather than an open-ended, creative journey at the loom? Was it simply because of design tradition? It was like having a pre-written score for classical music.

Why did the weaving switch to the back of the loom in the Middle Ages? So many workshops are still weaving from there today: Gobelin, Aubusson, and others.

Why are so many long mural tapestries still woven sideways, when the change from wooden looms to stronger metal looms removed this problem? The practice dates back to medieval times. For landscape shaped tapestries, from which of the two vertical edges does one start? Left to right or right to left? From the back? With a fine warp sett, in an era when the preferred warp count was 20/40 or even 80 warp ends per inch, and with sophisticated hatching techniques, a mural piece perhaps 12 feet wide by 30 feet long was rolled away on the bottom loom roller as the tapestry grew over months or years. How can weavers remember the earlier handling, color balance, and other decisions?

I have often asked tapestry conservators to examine the standard half-hitch start and finish of any shape or color. This would certainly tell us what was the start and finishing edge—left to right or right to left of the woven journey.

I design (as I weave) all my own tapestries now from rough sketches. For many years I have produced varied series of tapestries—-woven words, press photos, textiles of textiles, drawing, reconstruction (figures from medieval tapestries rewoven bottom to top with fewer warps), portraits, post cards, etc. I like to weave bottom to top shapes and create vertical pieces that can hang free, fixed only at the top edge, as opposed to the fixed four edges of a painted canvas—thereby exploring, and exploiting, the tapestry as a textile.

And, by the way, *hachure* is simply the French word for hatch.

–Archie Brennan

Exhibiting Changes

by Christine Laffer, Tapestry Artist, Writer, Curator

When a memory forms, it captures a series of spatial sensory effects and locks them into place. Location, sounds, time of day, movement, color, and even temperature leave notations that encapsulate a moment in time. In response to a trigger, you can relive that time, place, and event whether viewed frozen as a still frame or as a short replay of the past. We expect memories to stay in our heads as a resource, giving us a way to know who we are through what we have seen and done. History is essentially a composite of memories that many people transcribe again and again.

Tapestry has a complicated history. The current definition of a tapestry varies radically. In popular usage it can include a large tie-dyed cloth pinned on a wall, a small image made with colored threads and a needle, or a machine-woven reproduction of a romantic scene. Today we have access to a range of impressions from pictures, books, and film.

At the other end of the spectrum, museums showcase fifteenth- and sixteenth-century collections in their permanent galleries. Memories based on even a cursory visit to such museums fulfill the myth of tapestry as a frozen frame of the past rather than a changing, expanding universe of current creative production. This museum-authenticated version presents tapestry as a type of magnificent art seen in the context of Gothic and Renaissance eras. These collections have exerted great power by replicating themselves through the attention of historians and writers in popular media such as television, magazines, and the Internet. Stories and images constantly reiterate this baseline master tapestry form. If museums also hold collections of Coptic, Japanese, and Peruvian pieces, to mention a few other types, they relegate them to themed rooms separate from their European-art counterparts.

These acts of display perform a fixed view of tapestry directed at broad popular audiences, such as the 2002 exhibition "Tapestry in the Renaissance: Art and Magnificence" curated by Thomas Campbell at the Metropolitan Museum of Art. This exhibition garnered articles in the *New York Times* and clips on YouTube, as well as a TED Lecture with the curator in March 2012 (www.ted.com/talks/thomas_p_campbell_weaving_narratives_in_museum_galleries).

This method of repeating a particular view of history, as if tapestry did not exist outside that frame, does a great disservice to the reality. Many works made in a flat, dense fiber structure have developed into art forms in a wide variety of historical and contemporary cultures by artists of great skill and aesthetic sensibility.

If people are to see and remember tapestry as a broader art form, they must visit exhibitions by museums and galleries that have not invested heavily in collections obtained over a century ago. Contemporary displays are short term—less than 4 months—and contain pieces that do not come from prestigious or permanent collections and have only the authenticity of the artist's hand. Documentation provided by catalogs and local media can greatly extend the reach of these shows. Their impact on shared memory can't be compared to institutional collections. Each new exhibit must offer its audience a fresh starting point, because there is little chance to revisit it.

One significant exception to this power imbalance came in the early 1960s with the introduction of a biennial exhibition in Lausanne, Switzerland. At the end of World War II in Europe stood the figure of Jean Lurçat, an artist deeply committed to a view of tapestry rooted in the discovery of an unknown set of strikingly simple medieval works called the Apocalypse of Angers. He took the strengths of this large narrative format and recodified them into a method for producing new works for the post-war world. Lurçat traveled internationally as interest grew in his vision of tapestry as a participant in rebuilding our world. In 1961 he teamed up with Pierre Pauli, Paul-Henri Jaccard, Georges-André Chevallaz, and René Berger to form Le Centre Internationale de la Tapisserie Ancienne et Moderne. CITAM organized each of the fifteen Biennales de la Tapisserie Lausanne. Until its last exhibition in 1993, CITAM provided a central focus for developments taking place in textile art around the world.

The Lausanne Biennales marked more than a moment in changing the public view of tapestry. For thirty years it steadily offered a single location comparable to that of any historic collection with its immense wall space. It is difficult now to separate the changes in artistic direction from the exhibition itself. Few other exhibitions had the attention and competitive luster of this juried display that took over the Musée des Arts Décoratifs and later spilled into the streets. (In the early 1970s, other international textile art shows appeared, notably the International Triennial of Tapestry in Łódź, Poland.) Since it stood as the premier show against which others competed, jurors, artists, and organizers constantly argued over its name, direction, and methods of selection. (Taylor, 1983) As long as interest in fiber media surged, the show stood as a torchbearer signaling the future of textile art. When interest began to dissipate, possibly triggered by political and economic upheavals in Europe in the late 1980s, and as textile art took a pronounced conceptual turn, CITAM ceased its endeavor.

In contrast, American interest in fiber art took a slightly different path. Without a steady museum venue to host regular exhibitions and with very few private galleries dedicated to fiber works, artists relied on a disparate system of juried and invitational exhibitions, art agents, and various annual compendia publications to reach its audience. Influenced by the European biennials, American fiber artists established reputations abroad and then looked for private and corporate clients to commission works at home.

By 1982, as a counterpoint to the explosion of rapid advances occurring in fiber art forms, Hal Painter and Jim Brown had set up the American Tapestry Alliance (ATA) as a national organization to strengthen connections among far-flung tapestry weavers they had met and taught during their 1976 tour across the United States. They organized several exhibitions to share and promote the range of work they discovered by artist-weavers. The inaugural exhibition *Panorama of Tapestry*, 1986, included a piece by Jean Lurçat. This was followed by *World Tapestry Today* in 1988 and *American Tapestry Today* in 1990. Each exhibition traveled to several locations and was accompanied by a catalog.

Further, several independent curators mounted singular exhibitions. Courtney Ann Shaw organized *American Tapestry Weaving Since the 1930s and its European Roots* at The Art Gallery of the University of Maryland, College Park (1989). She pointed out the various weaving traditions (schools) that influenced the growth of tapestry in this country. The combined efforts of these independent exhibitions began to establish legitimacy for the developing American tapestry movement.

Helga Berry took up a broader undertaking as the result of her travels to centers of tapestry activity in Europe and the United States. By 1988 she had set up the International Tapestry Network (ITNET) for tapestry artists around the world. Not only did she print several volumes of the *ITNET Journal* but also initiated two large juried shows that traveled to several venues. *ITNET: Exhibit 1* occurred in 1990; *ITNET: Exhibit 2* in 1992; and *ITNET: Exhibit 3* in 1997. The latter exhibition existed only online and set a precedent as the first of its kind.

Four years after ITNET 2 and just three years after the last Lausanne Biennale, the ATA began its biennials, starting with the American Tapestry Biennial (ATB) in 1996. ATA continues to mount these international exhibitions, currently showing ATB 10. Each of their biennials appoints a different juror, conducts a public call for entries, and opens at three or four locations each cycle. In contrast to the record of controversy surrounding CITAM's selection process, both ITNET and ATA have incurred very little criticism, probably due to the stricter technical guidelines for qualification.

Outside of the ATA biennials, most display moments have resulted from the efforts of regional groups, primarily Tapestry Weavers West in the San Francisco Bay area, TWiNE in New England, and Tapestry Weavers South in the Southeast. However, the recent efforts of curators like Carol K. Russell here at the Hunterdon Art Museum suggest a renewed interest in tapestry in cultural areas enjoying a resurgence of urban life.

The very word *tapestry* connects us to an always-present past because of the depth of its institutional and cultural support system. Can one ever move completely away from the overwhelming shadow cast by 500-year-old exemplars such as The Hunt of the Unicorn tapestries, which our collective memory has accepted and endorsed? Modified terms such as "modern tapestry" and "contemporary tapestry" make this link to the past even more explicit. In fact, most contemporary artists who make time-intensive handwoven imagery try to underscore this relation to cultural memory. Many of them do not have any other touchstone for identifying and validating their artwork to a public audience.

A notable exception can be found in Navajo weaving. Those who developed their visual and technical abilities within a rich culture, without European references, had a specific and complex alternate system to draw upon in the trading posts and their evolution as large art fairs. No link to the word *tapestry* was necessary. Interestingly, the Navajo have a similar imbalanced relationship to historical collections made over the past 100 years, which wield high display power in cultural memory relative to contemporary work.

In terms of the power imbalance between contemporary artists and the large collections, the only arbiters who can actively influence this uneasy equilibrium are new collectors. They will build collections for the next 100 years as long as they have access to new work in shows such as this one.

–Christine Laffer

Christine Laffer, *Pacific Stock Exchange*, Handwoven tapestry: three-strand crewel wool yarn weft, cotton warp, 62 x 115" (155 x 288cm).

Embedded Narratives

A Canadian perspective on tapestry as a permeable and public art.

by Lycia Trouton, PhD

EPIGRAPH

Tapestries which have always been praised very highly have been affected by the changes in the social structure of our times. Tapestry was part of the art of living. The surface of a textile art work is ever-changing, giving it a living character.

—Ferdinand Eckhardt, upon the occasion of the Exhibition of the High Art of Tapestry Weaving. (Winnipeg, 1954, Preface, p. 3).

Dr. Lycia Trouton photographed outside the Cranbrook Museum, Academy of Art in front of a Harry Bertoia sculpture. Photo by Lisa Spindler

The tapestries of Barbara Heller, Ruth Jones, Jane Kidd, and Linda Wallace provide a road map of current Canadian art. Historically, as well as today, tapestry has the unique ability to embody the complex narratives about humankind over the millennia while creating a lasting archive for generations. (Gustafson, 1997, pp. 13-14) Tapestry and the applied or textile arts are seemingly in juxtaposition to the international reputation of another contemporary art practice from this Western region of Canada: The Vancouver School of photo-conceptualism. Yet to reflect on just how mainstreamed the *decorative* arts have become in recent years, we need only look to the work of Canada's representative to the 55th International Art exhibition at the Venice Biennale: Shary Boyle and her use of porcelain lace.

There are various definitions of tapestry, some more specific to contemporary North American creators/makers than others. While not tapestry in the strictest of Eurocentric definitions, exquisite weaving was one of the primary art forms of the northwest corner of Canada. Indigenous Coast Salish, Tlingit, and Tsimshian were weaving with the finest and softest, rare white mountain goat wool and the shredded inner bark of the cedar tree (Gustafson, 1997, p. 7, p. 10). Debra and Robyn Sparrow are two well-known contemporary practitioners of this art form thanks to a post-1980s cultural renaissance, following that of the already well-known Haida sculpture.

The discipline of *symbolic* tapestry has enjoyed new arts theory scholarship since the late 1960s along with feminism and soft sculpture (Wood Conroy, 1995) and a reinvigorated *postcolonial* lens since the mid-1990s (Trouton, 2005). Over this period, tapestry gained new credence as public art in public space and as community-based public art in regional areas in the Commonwealth countries such as Canada and Australia, forming a new generation of viewers and makers (Heller, 1997). The widely exhibited art of the Canadian talents upon which I focus--Heller, Jones, Kidd, Wallace—attests to their resilient careers as well as self and group advocacy over the period of the early 1980s to our current era.

Linda Wallace lives in a small community just north of Nanaimo, on Vancouver Island, British Columbia. As well as an artist, she's been an advocate for the tapestry arts with the determination of a Canadian pioneer-type of personality. Yet Wallace's seeming resilience in living a regional Canadian lifestyle need not mask her sensitive awareness to very cosmopolitan, current concerns to do with human vulnerability (medical issues) and environmental stressors. Her tapestry engages with socio-political concepts, which are sometimes portrayed in muted monochromes. At other times, Wallace uses graphic narrative with compelling color and the surprising insertion of dynamic metallic threads.

While Wallace has chosen solitary tapestry arts production and exhibition over her former "caring" career as a nurse, she is a global public figure in other ways as a writer, organizer, and speaker. Wallace takes on leadership roles in the art/textiles community in the American Tapestry Alliance as well as activities with British and Antipodean Tapestry groups. Additionally, she bravely places text into her artwork. Words like *evolve, reality, yearning, lamenting* are written in the artist's hand and placed or embedded into the art.

Barbara Heller spoke with me in person about the discipline of tapestry when I viewed her work in a Vancouver suburb, in a solo exhibition curated by Barbara Duncan. Heller is a towering founding figure in the West Coast Canadian movement for the legitimacy of tapestry since 1979. She weaves most days of the week in her "always-open-door-policy" studio on Granville Island, an infamous post-1980s Vancouver arts community and tourist destination.

Before her art journey with tapestry, Heller was a painter and printmaker with similar social justice (anti-war) and socio-political-environmental concerns. Heller's intellectual inquiry spans from historic content and technique to current concerns in tapestry. I was struck by Heller's risk-taking choice of the addition of miniature plastic litter *discards* in two of the five panels of *One Way*, 2013. As I am involved in art about grief and trauma, this detail seems to me to be a *memory* device related to contemporary deliberations in certain socio-political art between memory studies and the truth of history, as well as our constant questioning about context. This discard detail is a particularly good device with which to produce a feeling of fretting in her audience, perhaps forcing the need for concern, as does the larger pictorial narrative about the state of our ecology and wildlife.

Along with Barbara Heller, and of the same generation, Jane Kidd has been a passionate advocate of tapestry practice since 1979. Kidd has the distinction of being a member of the Royal Canadian Academy of Art and having been awarded the Alberta Craft Council Award of Excellence, 2008. Despite the bulk of her career in the academic environment in Alberta, Kidd—who has returned to her roots on the islands outside of Vancouver—also delights in the sensuous beauty and expressive capabilities of tapestry as *between* art and craft.

Ruth Jones, also of British Columbia, is known for her Aubusson methodology in tapestry. Jones' primary training was in classical studies, so it is with this background information that Jones seems refreshingly released from types of ambivalences that have plagued practitioners as a result of modernist training. The new postcolonial hybridism in textile arts in recent years has given way to a more open playing field and avenues for artistic achievement. The title of my essay privileges the idea of how imagery becomes *embedded* in the tapestry arts. Images in Jones' *Woad Diva* and *Jardin Palace* show, even in print, the qualities emblematic of her work, such as the play of light and dark in differing wool and silk threads, and pointillist coloring (Scott cited in Jones, 2012).

Jones has been part of a team weaving a recreation of *The Unicorn Tapestries*, with an educational link to The Cloisters, New York's Metropolitan Museum of Art, for Stirling Castle in Scotland. The project is funded by Historic Scotland, recalling the era of James V, fifteenth century. Jones directs the reweaving of the *Mystic Capture of the Unicorn* panel, from new digital research and a similarly themed existing woodblock print, because the original tapestry only exists in fragments (Jones cited in Mirzaghitova, 2013). Back in North America, a visitor to the Museum of Anthropology at the University of British Columbia, Vancouver is able to view one of Jones' original tapestries in the permanent collection. Jones uses the language of the body and musical or mathematical notation to lovingly describe her connection with her daily work in tapestry and artistic calling (Jones, 2012). The viewer, thus, also feels like *slipping into* her stories, made from hue, tone and elegant hachures.

It is rewarding to reflect upon how the fields of tapestry and textile conservation, as well as curating, have matured and expanded since the mid-1980s. New mandates, outlined in a 2008 United Kingdom research publication, *It's a material world: Caring for the public realm*, discuss the urgent need for new directions in the restoration arts. One of the ideas put forth in the document is to publicly *perform* conservation tasks, taking the invisibility of mending-in-conservation labs previously hidden from public view into public space, as well as into the public digital domain through blogging and tweeting, etc. Perhaps the legacy of community public art that engages needlework processes (Pershing, 1993), has extended to the fields of museology and conservation. There is a call for newly transparent and participatory site-specific processes. Only in these can both our individual and national identities, where the diversity of our present intercultural society meet, get full participation in the former ivory tower of museums, galleries, cultural heritage sites, and interpretation. It is a special moment for an individual to be able to think/feel that we can each, in our own way, *own* a story of reflection about an object such as a tapestry held in high esteem in an institutional collection. The talented and highly skilled tapestry artists in Canada—Wallace, Kidd, Heller, and Jones—link viewers to the living history of our times through this compellingly complex contemporary and ancient art form. It is my hope that my essay may have helped lead you through a perspective into the next tapestry garden of your choice and enjoy this book.

-Lycia Trouton, PhD

Introduction to Contemporary International Tapestry

Curated by Carol K. Russell

Welcome to our world: the world of tapestry art and a world of art in tapestry. The word *tapestry* brings to mind romantic music, images of mythical beasts, and the ornate styles and surroundings of nobility. At this point in time tapestry has flown past and far beyond its own visual history. The three generations of artists in this exhibition view art itself taking precedence over the woven cloth as they impose *their* tunes upon the dance of the loom. An ancient medium survives in the hands and minds of practitioners with no intention of rigidly continuing past conventions but rather inventing their own styles and signing tapestries with their own names. This 2015 exhibition at the Hunterdon Art Museum in Clinton, New Jersey, showcases three generations of tapestry artists from nine countries.

Though each artist may follow the simple over and under woven structure of tapestry, practiced since the beginning of time, they arrive at this exhibition from far-flung cultures and influences we in New Jersey can only imagine and hope to share. One might assert that *tapestry is tapestry* worldwide, but that would dismiss influences such as national weaving traditions, regional tapestry studios, universities with excellent textile arts programs, even beloved teachers. Exhibited here are works by tapestry's great masters, mentors, gurus, and of course their protégées. Lessons involved much more than weaving instruction. Finding one's voice in a pile of colored threads requires working under an experienced practitioner with words of wisdom delivered in tapestry's unique vocabulary.

Lore Kadden Lindenfeld and Silvia Heyden are represented by works born of their studies with renowned Bauhaus teachers Joseph and Anni Albers and Johannes Itten. The Albers came to Black Mountain College in North Carolina from Germany after Hitler closed the Bauhaus in 1933. For those displaced, and for the American avant-garde of that era, Black Mountain became a haven. Lore Lindenfeld arrived there from Cambridge, Massachusetts, where her family settled after emigrating from Germany. Silvia Heyden had the benefit of Itten's post-war Bauhaus teachings at the School of Arts in Zurich, Switzerland. Indeed, Itten himself saw relationships between music and color in a manner similar to Silvia Heyden—an accomplished violinist.

During the worst of times in world history these young artists blazed pathways to achievement. Worth noting was the traditional Bauhaus limitation on women artists being taught only the gentler arts: notably weaving. Yet, what better way to examine Bauhaus color theories and constructivist principles than at a loom with living inventors of a new arts movement.

> Though I am dealing in this book with long-established facts and processes, still, in exploring them, I feel on new ground. And just as it is possible to go from any place to any other, so also, from a defined and specialized field, can one arrive at a realization of ever-extending relationships. Thus tangential subjects come into view. The thoughts, however, can, I believe, be traced back to the event of a thread.
>
> —Anni Albers from On Weaving, by Anni Albers

Artist and curator Dirk Holger trained in France at the Aubusson Tapestry School and continued as the last assistant to tapestry legend Jean Lurçat (1892-1966). Today he organizes exhibitions to promote interest in the art that has been his life. Though the content of Holger's imagery is now more personal, his mentor's distinctive visual presence flows like a river from generation to generation.

> It was the genius of Jean Lurçat that turned tapestry's fate around. Inspired by the Apocalypse d'Angers, Lurçat revived the essence of tapestry as an autonomous art form by reviving its spirit.
> —Dirk Holger

Jean Pierre Larochette and Yael Lurie brought classic French Aubusson backgrounds in art and tapestry-making skills to the San Francisco Tapestry Workshop in the 1970s. Working with designs by Yael, Mark Adams, Judy Chicago (with weaver Audrey Cowan), and other artists of that era, the studio turned out original tapestries in the Aubusson style while training art students in its collaborative approach. Many professional tapestry artists, now with their own independent practices, sustain their Larochette and Lurie influences. A community was created and a new movement begun from a medieval European idiom that evolves still today. Amongst those striking out on their own with the lessons of the masters in their hearts and minds are Constance Hunt, Helga Berry, Christine Laffer, Julia Mitchell, and Elizabeth Buckley.

Helga Berry went on to co-found ITNET along with San Francisco Tapestry Workshop colleague Christine Laffer. Well traveled but always returning home to her inspiring Alaskan landscapes, Helga organized touring exhibitions that sent forth tapestries and catalogs showcasing international and American tapestry talents of the 1990s. Participating artists appreciated such opportunities for showing their work in a juried international context. Given the fresh look of newer works selected, increased interest in tapestry on the part of museums, galleries, and collectors continued into the new century. Individuality of style was highlighted. The tapestry movement became magnetic and worthy art followed. This exhibition at the Hunterdon Art Museum sustains the concept of *art museum as forum* for contemporary tapestry.

Helga Berry. *Two Heads, One Mind.* Handwoven tapestry: silk, wool, metallic, and synthetic fibers. 8 x 8" (15 x 15cm). Photo: Chris Arend Photography.

> There is a link between the public exhibition of art and its value.
> —From the catalog *ITNET: Exhibit 2* by Professor Janis Jefferies, artist, critic, lecturer, and curator: University of London.

Then as now, international exhibitions are vital to developing an art history and body of critique for contemporary tapestry. Shedding much of tapestry's orthodox past, the Lausanne Biennial exhibitions began in earnest in 1962 to establish art in the textile medium as constituent to fine arts. Unsustainable by the mid-1990s, the Lausanne exhibitions nevertheless generated sufficient interest in collective presentations of art textiles to inspire international shows in Łódź, Poland; Beijing, China; Como, Italy; Portneuf, Canada; and other destinations. Interestingly, many such sites have textile-making histories, adding enrichment to the main exhibition events.

The *Międzynarodowe Triennale Tkaniny* (*International Triennial of Tapestry*) at the Centralne Muzeum Włókiennictwa (Central Museum of Textiles in Łódź, Poland), soon to open its fifteenth iteration, honors a range of works by Polish and international textile artists. Reinventing tapestry's classic structure, Polish artist Włodzimierz Cygan presents here his seemingly impossible spherical and angular gestures. Describing emotional extremes and dark, infinite spaces, his loom and materials are clearly in the service of *his* expressions. Ewa Latkowska-Żychska takes inspiration from Poland's natural world where she lives, weaves, and writes her poetry. Born and educated in Polish textile traditions, New Jersey's Bojana Leznicki reflects a tapestry spirituality inspired by abstract prayers. There is much to appreciate and share with the post-war generation of Polish tapestry artists.

Spirituality also forms the foundation upon which Soyoo Park Caltabiano weaves reflections of her interesting life divided between South Korea and New Jersey. Native American Ramona Sakiestewa captures abstract images and colors from the earth and sky of her New Mexico home. Ina Golub's tapestries embrace and celebrate her Jewish spirituality through the rituals, stories, and poems of her people. Elizabeth Buckley's *Veil* could refer to a face covering or in her words ". . .wind's movement can lift the curtain that separates one realm from another." Lialia Kuchma's *Luke I* connects tidings from the *Bible*'s Old Testament to the New. Ruth Jones alludes to a "mysterious resonance" in her work. Given tapestry's unusual concentration of mind, eye, and hand, few art forms so thoroughly absorb, then reflect, the true spirit or *resonance* of its maker.

> Art after all is but an extension of language to the expression of sensations too subtle for words. And we will acquire this greater power of revealing ourselves.
> —Robert Henri, from *The Art Spirit*, Harper & Row

Exploring the art spirit are students of Archie Brennan and Susan Martin Maffei, who hold classes in their studio for a select group of New York and New Jersey tapestry enthusiasts. Together in life and art, Archie and Susan work with students ready to add personal refinements to their designs while sharing the tapestry values, experiences, and accomplishments of their mentors.

Born in Scotland, Archie's background includes graduate and post-graduate studies at Edinburgh College of Art and apprenticeship, then directorship, at Dovecot Studios, a one-hundred-year-old tapestry studio in Edinburgh. Appointed Officer of the British Empire (OBE) by Queen Elizabeth II for his contribution to the arts, Archie will be honored again at the National Museum of Scotland with a retrospective exhibition marking his eighty-fifth birthday. Archie has entertained and enriched us over the years with his engaging tapestries reflecting personal and often intellectual responses to history, culture, and even art itself.

Susan interned at the French tapestry workshop *Manufacture Nationale des Gobelins* in Paris followed by an apprenticeship and studio work at Scheuer Tapestry Studio in NYC. Susan weaves views of New York, its human and animal populations, and its unique geometric rhythms. Though tapestries are often considered *grand,* this artist prefers the richness of everyday people in the dramas of their urban pursuits.

Recently, she produced *Narratives: Tapestries Designed and Woven by Susan Martin Maffei,* an artist's book of her large-scale tapestries. Susan writes in her book: "The early history of tapestry making has always evoked a narrative of the surrounding world of human existence."

Narrations in tapestry portray much more than two-dimensional stories. The unique vitality of obviously heavy cloth has inspired new waves of invention in the old medium. Imagery may confront or critique other visual experiences.

Barbara Heller. *Eritrean Refugees*. Handwoven tapestry: wool, linen, and silk on linen warp. 35 x 25" (80 x 79cm). Photo Ted Clarke: Image This.

Barbara Heller's *Eritrean Refugees* are compelled to live in cloth tents. With cloth they cover their faces and bodies according to the dictates of religion, yet undernourished women are clearly exposed by too-thin hands and forearms. Joan Baxter's response to 9/11 positions her loom on the shore of Scotland facing westward toward New York. Implied are Scots and Americans interwoven in disbelief and compassion. With refreshing candor, Sarah Swett weaves glimpses of a past life in *Casting Off,* considered not with regret but with better ideas woven in bright new colors. Micala Sidore's tapestry series *Black & White & Red All Over* explores letters and words in clever alternative contexts suggesting messages within messages, double entendres, or irony in language.

In addition to *Watershed* by Yael Lurie and Jean Pierre Larochette, this exhibition was blessed with several submissions on thoughts of water, a huge concern in these times to humans who live near water, swim in it, drink it, or enjoy its delicious bounty. In New Jersey, we live with epic stories of water's power from both our east and westward edges. As with others worldwide, we witness water's life-giving elements with traces of fear. Germany's Peter Horn presents a grim view of ancient stone faces on *Easter Island* as water levels rise. Canada's Barbara Heller allows escape for neither birds nor man as rising water and toxic materials fill city streets in her tapestry *One Way*. Also from Canada, Jane Kidd presents a series of tapestries comparing findings from the natural world preserved and displayed along with bits and pieces of material culture. Marking these *Possessions* is a human fingerprint in the lower right corner. Linda Wallace weaves lovely Canadian birds responding to environmental distress. From a different angle, California's Janet Moore weaves a mighty river flowing peacefully through earth's bounty at either edge. As always, views of the times are reflected in tapestries of the times.

Recognizable objects or places often carry symbolic overtones with no specific story in mind but rather as memories or feelings. A red barn in Denmark by Lise DeCoursin marks both a tangible childhood place and how she remembers it still. Susan Edmunds cast forever in woven tapestry her impressions of intricately composed stones on an island off the coast of Ireland. Alla Davydova recalls in tapestry her view of Russia's political history and also dear family members photographed during happy times. Suggestions of human imagery appear in Susan Iverson's *Dream Sequence* along with glimpses of the *dream* described in abstract. Susan Hart Henegar captures the energy, grace, and free spirit of colorful horses. A very different sort of abstract horse appears symbolically in Aino Kajaniemi's tapestry *Sounder*.

In tapestry, as in other fine art mediums, abstraction lends itself to the development of distinctive and readily recognizable styles. Jon Eric Riis begins with accessible forms: a human body or a garment never intended to be worn. At first glance, one notices a fluent and gracefully presented object; closer inspection reveals insightful and thought-provoking content. Rebecca Bluestone's abstract mountains and landscapes communicate the purest forms and colors of the American Southwest. Alex Friedman manipulates her tapestry's underlying structure giving visible form to abstract rhythms. Elinor Steele deconstructs shapes and images until they are no longer recognizable, then reorganizes them into a new composition with strength and balance. Jo Barker, with an almost playful spontaneity, leads a viewer into and through her emotive space to ponder its ambiguity.

To tapestry artists, there is no absolute distinction between major and minor arts. We all practice fine art. We imagine a tapestry, manifest our thoughts in a color medium, and prepare a cartoon to direct the weaving toward its finished dimensions. A cartoon is a rendering of a preliminary design to the scale of the finished tapestry.

Meet the artists who have sent their tapestries to Clinton, New Jersey, from their colorful studios in countries as far away as Russia and as nearby as Canada and Mexico. We are as different as the sounds of our voices and as similar as our passion for quiet hours at the loom. There is no magic in a loom. Its apparent humbleness and simplicity stand in stark contrast to the weaver's hands and eyes directing a million marks of imagination. A loom is simply a universally understood system for exploring oneself, which is an impossible thing to counterfeit.

A final thought: Never ask a tapestry artist, "How long did it take to weave this tapestry?" He or she will respond quite correctly, "It took my entire life up to the point at which this tapestry was cut from the loom, and the same for the next tapestry and the ones after that!

–Carol K. Russell

HOMAGE TO JOANNE JENSDATTER

There is a small sign in the midst of a weaving display in Oslo, Norway, giving recognition to a sixteenth century woman, who having fled her studio for the Norwegian coast, was burned to death for wanting to weave tapestry, which was at that time an exclusively male pursuit. None of her work survived. Her life story impacted me, for I am Norwegian, I am a woman, I weave tapestry, and my grandfather sailed to America from that same port town of Bergen.

I began researching. According to Norse mythology, the *Fabric of Life* was woven by the three Norns with a thread for each person: brown for farmers-workers, gold-silver for royalty, and a colored thread for each poet, musician, writer, and artist. Butterflies not only symbolize transformation and resurrection, they also are the name of the figure-eight bobbins used by weavers. In my tapestry she is reaching for a butterfly bobbin of colored silk.

The borders are sixteenth century designs. The tapestry is mounted on burned wood so one can experience the scent of fire. For you, Joanne, I wove an Homage piece. Joanne Jensdatter, Norsk weaver burned to death in 1594.

–Constance Hunt, tapestry artist

Constance Hunt. *Homage to Joanne Jensdatter.* Handwoven tapestry: cotton warp cotton, wool weft; mixed media: burned wood, antique bobbins, space-dyed silk. 16 x 10.5" (40 x 25.5cm). Photo: Gary Hunt.

The Artists

Jo Barker
Edinburgh, Scotland

With tapestries in collections such as the Victoria & Albert Museum, London; the House of Lords, London; and the Royal Victory Infirmary, Newcastle, UK; Jo Barker continues to develop her singular abstract style creating unique experiences according to the viewer's perceptions. The vibrant surface of her tapestry delivers a luminous release of energy seemingly impossible with only fine threads woven into a recognizable textile. One feels the tactile surface of the object without having to touch it. Here is abstract tapestry in its own time. Not a picture but sensitive layers of emotional responses to be peeled away during an unhurried visit. The colors of her threads sing of chromatic vibrations; her tangible strokes of shimmering yarns lure a viewer into deeper mindscapes—hers or yours?

> The medium of tapestry has a unique presence and sensuality. For me it lends itself to the use of intense color and provides a richness of surface texture which is very different from paint. Once a woven fabric is made from the yarns, the light is absorbed rather than reflected, creating a far denser, more sumptuous quality.
>
> —Jo Barker

Jo Barker. *Ellipse III.* Handwoven tapestry: cotton warp with wool, cotton, linen, silk, and metallic embroidery threads. 50 x 67" (127 x 170cm). Private collection.

Joan Baxter

Brora, Sutherland, Scotland

Summerstones is the main piece in a series of tapestries inspired by my first visit to the Orkney Islands. I'd read about Orkney's magnificent archaeological remains for years and felt as if I knew what these famous sites would look and feel like, but no photograph can prepare you for how the stones of Stenness and Brodgar sit into their landscape so modestly, so comfortably. My first thought, when I saw the stones from a distance, was that they seem to staple the land and the water to the sky; they are the joining element. When you get close up their size creates a different response, they tower over you and each stone seems to have a distinct personality. This tapestry was originally an attempt to show both these responses in the one composition.

I was about halfway up the tapestry when the terrible events of the 11th of September 2001, occurred. Immediately I knew that whatever I had originally intended this tapestry to be, it must now also become a response to the event. None of what I wove from that day on was consciously redesigned or thought through in any way, I just wove. So instead of a plain border with the shadow of the big stone within it, I found myself weaving clouds of solid-looking smoke with the two towers behind and through the ancient stone. The juxtaposition seemed right but I have no idea what it might mean. If it does say something profound, then it is beyond words.

—Joan Baxter 2014

My work deals with landscape, its echoes of history, its legends, its atmospheres and moods. I am particularly inspired by the rich cultural heritage and wild beauty of the landscapes of the far north of Scotland where I live.

I choose to work in the traditional woven tapestry medium because I like the way my initial ideas can develop and expand during the slow and deliberate making process.

The process, although a very ancient one, allows me to push boundaries in design, technique, materials, and concepts.

—Joan Baxter

Joan Baxter. *Summerstones.*
Handwoven tapestry. 22 x 258"
(55 x 655cm)

Helga Berry

Anchorage, Alaska, USA

Hat by fiber artist Lucy Zercher, Chugiak, AK.

As co-founder and president of ITNET (International Tapestry Network), Helga Berry has spread awareness of contemporary tapestry far beyond her home in Alaska. Gathering prominent international artists never before exhibited in the United States, she produced museum exhibitions emphasizing tapestry as fine art, very fine art indeed! The long-term results of these efforts continue to serve a global tapestry community increasingly appreciative of this ancient practice.

Born in Germany, Helga studied at the *Manufactures Nationales des Gobelins* in Paris where she experienced the high warp tapestry techniques refined and sustained there since 1662. Underpinned with solid European tapestry standards and an uncompromising artistic sensibility, her heart and mind engaged fully with the active west-coast tapestry movement in her adopted country.

Helga's tapestries have been exhibited in international venues such as: 10th Triennale of Tapestry, Central Museum of Textiles, Łódź, Poland; Miniartextil; Como, Italy; International Biennale of Miniature Textiles, Szombathely, Hungary; and the Miniature Textile exhibit, Kulturni Center Misko Kranjec, Murska Sobota, Yugoslavia.

Helga Berry. *Meditation.* Handwoven tapestry: silk metallic and synthetic fibers. 8 x 7" (20 x 18cm). Photo: Chris Arend Photography.

Helga Berry. *Becoming Predestined.* Handwoven tapestry: wool, silk, metallic, and synthetic fibers. 68 x 68" (173 x 173cm). Photo: Chris Arend Photography.

Rebecca Bluestone

Santa Fe, New Mexico, USA

With tapestries in prestigious museum collections such as New York City's Museum of Art and Design (MAD), Chicago Art Institute and the Denver Art Museum, Rebecca Bluestone emphasizes with special pride her works placed worldwide through the Art in Embassies program. Initiated in 1964 by President John F. Kennedy and his wife, Jacqueline, the program promotes a sense of cultural identity through America's art and artists.

I have participated in the Art in Embassies program for many years, loaning work to embassies from Taiwan to Africa. The US Embassies in Ottawa, Canada; and Quito, Ecuador; have my work in their permanent collections. Since I strongly believe that visual art speaks about those aspects of human experience for which we have no words, it becomes a universal language, crossing economic, racial, political, religious, and cultural divisions. What better form of communication is there?

I am a contemporary abstract artist. For my medium, I use traditional tapestry techniques and hand-dyed silks of varied textures and sheens along with metallic threads woven on a cotton warp. Instead of applying paint to canvas, I dye the fibers first and then, in essence, weave my own canvas. This creates a tactile, immediate surface that interacts with light in a very unique way. Working with the language of color, I use hundreds of color combinations in each of my pieces. Applying the chiaroscuro effect of balancing light and dark, I attempt to illuminate the space between the interior and exterior landscapes of life.

—Rebecca Bluestone

Rebecca Bluestone. *Landscape series: triptych #2*. Handwoven tapestry: silk, dyes, metallic thread on cotton warp. 61 x 72" (152.5 x 180cm). Photo: Addison Doty.

Archie Brennan

New Baltimore, New York, USA

The tapestry *Monsieur Bonnard's Grand Daughter* is number 357 of the total of 498 I have designed and woven to date (not counting miniatures) since 1953. It is number 89 (LXXXIX) of my drawing series, based on one of the many hundreds of life drawings from my weekly practice of drawing from the model—around the world—since 1947.

I weave tapestries in series: woven words, reconstructed details from early European tapestries, postcards, Dersu Uzala, textiles, Muhammad Ali Series, newspaper images, etc.

This *Bonnard* tapestry was so called because the woven "frame" was a frame Pierre Bonnard used for many of his paintings. I wove this tapestry in Paris in 2001 when Susan and I spent some months there and saw a particular Bonnard exhibition. The "Grand Daughter" is in fact based on a drawing of mine made in Hawaii around 1990.

Why the "erased" features? It was simply that when I made the drawing I struggled with, and then erased, the features. I used this when I wove the tapestry, so that the female was anonymous and simplified. Such a decision is because the only person I seek to satisfy in my work is me.

—Archie Brennan on *Monsieur Bonnard's Grand Daughter*

Archie Brennan.
Monsieur Bonnard's Grand Daughter.
Handwoven tapestry. 40 X 30.5" (100 X 76cm).

Elizabeth J. Buckley

Albuquerque, New Mexico, USA

Elizabeth J. Buckley's approach to the art of tapestry involves working in multiple layers and dimensions to create visual poems of blended colors and light. Thematic in her work is the undercurrent of time in terms of millennia; time of the forces which molded Earth's canyons and mesas, oceans and mountains; time filled with the spirits of those who have come before.

Her *Veil Tapestries* reference the drape of fabric often depicted in classic, historic French tapestry, and describe how wind's movement can lift the curtain that separates one realm from another. Over the years, Elizabeth's work has evolved from using techniques of the Mexican and Rio Grande traditions to those of French tapestry. She studied with Jean Pierre Larochette and Yael Lurie, and then further honed her skills in Aubusson, France, at the atelier of Gisèle Brivet. Elizabeth prefers to work in the Aubusson tradition for her larger works. She is devoted to being a lineage-keeper of these vanishing techniques, not only through her own tapestries, but also in her teaching. In her classes she demonstrates how design principles and color theory relate to tapestry-making. She draws from multiple tapestry traditions to provide her students with the technique vocabulary for finding and expressing their own unique voice.

DIALOGUES THROUGH THE VEIL

The space between now and then
Opens
Like a window
Into the moment,
Inviting the presence of
Mary, the poet,
Ann, the peacemaker,
And so many others,
To leave traces
Of their thoughts
In these threads.

Currents of time and air
Flow
Into this veil of mist and memory;
This waterfall of light
On cottonwood leaves
Beside my studio.

400 hours made visible,
Like beach patterns of ocean on sand.

— Poem by Elizabeth J. Buckley

Elizabeth Buckley. *Dialogues Through the Veil*. Handwoven Aubusson-style tapestry: mothproofed wool, silk and cotton on cotton warp. 48 x 25" (122cm x 64cm). Photo: Lany Eila.

Soyoo Park Caltabiano

South Korea and Demarest, New Jersey, USA

Soyoo Park Caltabiano, an artist in various visual media, teacher, and author and illustrator of children's books, emigrated in 1986 from Seoul, South Korea. There was no tradition of tapestry weaving in her homeland but a strong movement in fiber arts that continues still today. Her MFA from Hong-Ik University prepared her for life as an artist in America, though she still needed to refine weaving techniques for translating her designs into tapestries. Interestingly, she experimented with and adopted the same techniques mastered by the French Gobelins weavers centuries ago.

> On completion of the first sixty-year cycle of my life according to the Asian Zodiac, I am preparing for a more meaningful sixty years to come.
>
> The bicycle wheel gave me the idea of depicting two aspects of life. In the repetition of everyday life and meditation while weaving, I see a pattern. In the past I've depicted in my tapestries the physical world. Now I'm showing the movement in my mind.
>
> My weaving is intuitive with little planning. My five tapestries *Cycles of Life* are 1. Sun in my Heart: Yin, Yang; 2. Moon in my Mind: Giving, Receiving; 3. Touched by People, Touched by God; 4. Cage: Question: "Are you having fun or are you afraid to come out?" Answer: "I think I am myself and I am a part of nature"; 5. Beyond.
>
> This approach led me to ponder the relationship of my life to the outside world. I'm still questioning my place in it.
>
> —Soyoo Park Caltabiano

Soyoo Park Caltabiano. *Cycles of Life: Sun in my Heart: Yin*. Handwoven tapestry: mercerized cotton, wool, and metallic cord on cotton warp. 25" diameter x 6" depth (62.5 x 15cm).

Soyoo Park Caltabiano. *Cycles of Life: Sun in my Heart: Yang* (detail).

Soyoo Park Caltabiano. *Cycles of Life: Sun in my Heart: Yang* (detail).

Soyoo Park Caltabiano. *Cycles of Life: Moon in my Mind.* Handwoven tapestry: mercerized cotton, wool, and metallic cord on cotton warp. 25" diameter x 6" depth (62.5 x 15cm).

Soyoo Park Caltabiano.
Cycles of Life: Touched by People. Handwoven tapestry: mercerized cotton, wool, and metallic cord on cotton warp. 21" diameter x 6" depth (52.5 x 15cm).

Soyoo Park Caltabiano.
Cycles of Life: Cage.
Handwoven tapestry: mercerized cotton, wool, and metallic cord on cotton warp. 23" diameter x 6" depth (52.5 x 15cm).

Włodzimierz Cygan

Łódź, Poland

Always on the cutting edge of tapestry and textile architecture, Polish artist Włodzimierz Cygan continues to reinvent his medium and his messages. Such talent has been rewarded with the Bronze Medal at the 6th International Fiber Art Biennial *From Lausanne to Beijing*, Zhengzhou, China. His tapestry *Orbitrek* earned the Grand Prix at the 12th International Triennial of Tapestry in Łódź, Poland.

> The goal of the project is an attempt to restore the organizing function of tapestry in a space while preserving its artistic autonomy. To create and search for unique relationships between tapestry, the wall, and space with the aid of technical means such as LED lighting and light-conducting fiber PMMA. To achieve full expression I use the woven forms of expressive silhouettes while their holes, cracks, and slits show the viewer what is behind them. I vary the shape of the outer contour to connect the object with its background. I intend for my work to be subjected to modulated variability, though excessively not absorbing the viewer's attention nor dissipating his or her contact with the object; to be so little different in every next moment, for each glance. Such a plan enables a merger of two qualities: the materiality of the tapestry with the immateriality of light: material durability with constantly changing context.
>
> —Quoted from Włodzimierz Cygan's catalog *Po-Światy* from the essay by Małgorzata Markiewicz Wróblewska, Senior Curator, Head of the Department of Textile Art in the Central Museum of Textiles, Łódź, Poland. Translation by Marzena Ziejka

Włodzimierz Cygan. *Dear Astrid I.*
Handwoven tapestry: wool, sisal, optical fiber.
98 x 16" (245 x 40cm).

Włodzimierz Cygan. *Dear Astrid I* (detail).

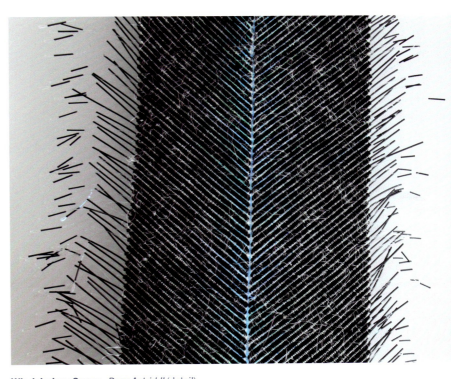

Włodzimierz Cygan. *Dear Astrid II* (detail).

Włodzimierz Cygan. *Dear Astrid II*.
Handwoven tapestry: wool, sisal,
optical fiber. 98 X 16" (245 x 40cm).

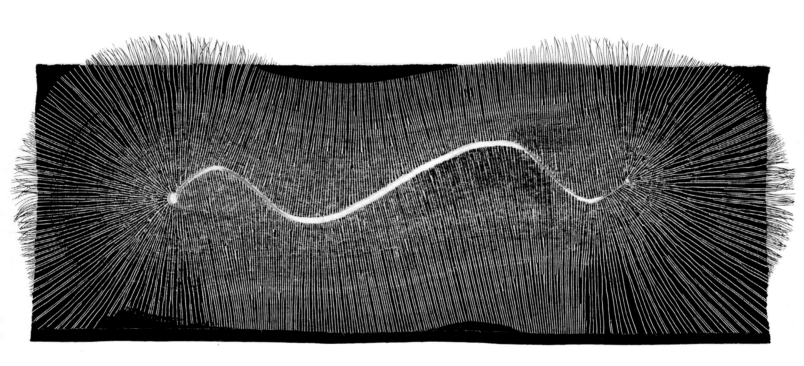

Włodzimierz Cygan. *Orbitrek.* Handwoven tapestry: wool, sisal. 39 x 118" (97.5 x 295cm).

Alla Davydova

St. Petersburg, Russia

Drawing on a depth of Russian history and culture, Alla Davydova has woven large-scale tapestry commissions for the Central Hotel in Kaliningrad, the Museum of the City of Samara, and the Pulkovskaya Hotel in St. Petersburg. More recently, her tapestries explore personal points of view on the history she has lived.

Reflecting the artist's signature abstract style, her tapestry *Mirage* suggests fragments of urban structures, streets, landscapes, fields streaked with red, and a central window accessed along a white pathway. Following the pathway one encounters dark places and deep fractures.

Memory becomes apparent again as the artist draws inspiration from a family photo album. Her small-scale tapestries portray children dressed in their best clothing while posed in rigid formal settings. The children's poses and settings are strikingly similar to photographs of the same era (1930s through the 1950s) from European and American family albums. Familiar as well are the artificial colors interrupting here and there the faded neutral tones of the photographs. During the earlier decades of film cameras it was common practice to highlight hair ribbons or other features in a black and white print with transparent touches of dyes. Recreated in tapestry, these genre images of children could be our own cousins.

Alla Davydova. *Mirage.* Handwoven tapestry: wool, silk, mixed fibers. 44 x 42" (110 x 105 cm).

Alla Davydova. *Brothers.* Handwoven tapestry: wool. 28 x 24" (70 x 60 cm).

Alla Davydova. *Girl Sitting on a Chair.* Handwoven tapestry: wool, silk. 28 x 24" (70 x 60 cm).

Lise DeCoursin

North Caldwell, New Jersey, USA

Violin case in hand, Lise DeCoursin emigrated as a young woman from her native Denmark to the United States. After music studies at Oberlin Conservatory of Music, she expanded her artistic inclinations into the realm of visual art. Lise's sensitivity for bringing forth classical music on an instrument with strings served her well in playing the strings of her tapestry loom. With amazing acuity and a rare discipline already in place, she sought out master tapestry artists Archie Brennan and Susan Martin Maffei for studies. Her tapestry of St. Nicholas as Russian icon was exhibited at the White Nights International Symposium in St. Petersburg, Russia.

Landscapes and the natural world most inspire her: the Danish seacoast as it turns that special blue against the pink flowers on the beach; a full moon shining on the wings of a luna moth; her terrified cat.

Lise DeCoursin. *My Cat Wally*. Handwoven tapestry: wool weft on cotton warp. 23 x 18" (57.5 x 45cm).

Lise DeCoursin. *The Red Barn*. Handwoven tapestry: wool, DMC cotton on cotton warp. 25 x 29" (62.5 x 72.5cm).

Lise DeCoursin. *Moon Flight*. Handwoven tapestry: wool, DMC cotton on cotton warp. 26 x 19" (65 x 47.5cm).

Susan T. Edmunds

Highland Park, New Jersey, USA

In 1976 I received a PhD in classics from Harvard University. Subsequently, I was employed as a teacher of Greek and Latin, then editor, publications director, technical writer, test developer, and teacher of Iyengar yoga. I came to weaving relatively late in life and, as a weaver, was brought back to my earlier studies of Greek antiquity, becoming curious about ancient textile practices. In 2005, I co-produced a DVD, *Text & Textile: an Introduction to Wool-Working for Readers of Greek and Latin*. My article "Picturing Homeric Weaving" appears in an online volume honoring Gregory Nagy on the website of the Center for Hellenic Studies in Washington, D.C.

Aran Islands Kilim was inspired by the stone walls of the Aran Islands, Ireland, the eloquence of the hands that built and rebuilt them over the centuries, and the wildflowers, light, and water that surround them.

In weaving Kilim-style, I seek to honor the horizontal line, the simplest design element of any weft-faced woven structure. In Aran Islands Kilim, as in the dry-laid walls on the Aran Islands, any verticality is the result of stacking and balancing.

—Susan T. Edmunds

Susan Edmunds. *Aran Islands Kilim*. Handwoven tapestry: wool weft on wool warp. Weft is hand-dyed with plant dyes except for grays, which are commercially dyed. 51 x 45" (127.5 x 112.5cm). Photo: Maria Pondopoulo.

Susan Edmunds. *Aran Islands Kilim* (detail).

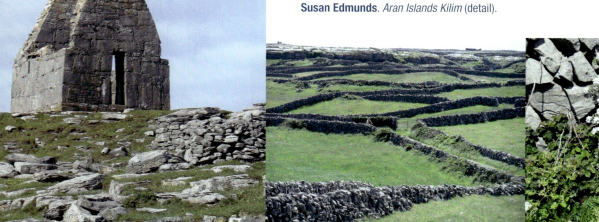

Susan Edmunds. *Aran Islands Kilim* (inspiration).

Alexandra Schilling Friedman

Sausalito, California, USA

While working in an architectural office as a model builder, Alex Friedman took an evening weaving class at the YWCA and became instantly fascinated with the many possibilities of woven textiles. Her enthusiasm landed her a job in New York City weaving shaped tapestries for the bulkheads of Pan Am 747s.

From that point on, she has maintained an active tapestry studio, making commissions, exhibiting, teaching, lecturing on tapestry, serving as panelist at a Tapestry Design Symposium in Washington, D.C, and becoming a finalist in the Kate Derum Award Show at the Australian Tapestry Workshop in Melbourne, Australia. With opportunities to live abroad and travel to many places, she seeks out the textiles of a region in the belief that they are the truest expression of a local culture.

> I have woven many tapestries over the years and considered each one a construction project that begins at the foundation and builds upwards.
>
> Rather than focus on the narrative element of traditional tapestries, my interest in exploring the third dimension evolved by playing with tension so I could create a surface that moves dynamically, as well as provides an energetic design.
>
> —Alex Friedman

Alex Friedman. *Flow 6.* Handwoven tapestry: wool weft on cotton warp. 55 x 35 x 2" (137.5 x 87.5 x 5cm). Photo: Craig Kolb.

Ina Golub

Mountainside, New Jersey, USA

The book of Exodus eloquently describes the making of the accoutrements of the Sanctuary, all to be made by the artist Bezalel, in the shadow of God. Each time I read these pages anew, my inner voice speaks, compelling me to pursue the creation of yet another ceremonial form, be it a monumental project that considers a total architectural environment, a garment worn by a rabbi or cantor, a sculptural form that may turn into a fanciful megillah scroll, or a spice container crafted of the tiniest beads. As an artist, I feel privileged to create in the shadow of God.

—Ina Golub, from her exhibition *The Work of the Weaver in Colors*. Yeshiva University Museum, New York, NY.

Ina Golub. *Views of the Old City*. Handwoven tapestry: wool on cotton warp. 31 X 58.5" (77.5 X 146cm). On loan from Temple Emanu-El, Westfield, NJ.

An Arab Shepherd is Searching for His Goat on Mount Zion

An Arab shepherd is searching for his goat on Mount Zion
And on the opposite hill I am searching for my little boy.

An Arab shepherd and Jewish father
Both in their temporary failure.

Our two voices met above
The Sultan's Pool in the valleys between us.

Neither of us wants the boy or the goat
To get caught in the wheels
Of the "Had Gadya" machine.

Afterwards we found them among the bushes,
And our voices came back inside us
Laughing and crying.

Searching for a goat or for a child has always been
The beginning of a new religion in these mountains.

—By Yehuda Amichai (1924-2000), considered Israel's greatest modern poet.

Ina Golub. *My Secret Place*. Handwoven tapestry: wool on cotton warp, 10 x 5' (305 X 152cm), Private Collection. Photo: Erik Landsberg.

Ina Golub. *The World is Based on Three Things… Torah, Worship and Loving Deeds*. Handwoven tapestry: wool on cotton warp. Height 25" (62.5cm). Torah Mantle for Chapel, Congregation Beth Am, Los Altos Hills, CA. Photo: Taylor Photo.

Barbara Heller

Vancouver, British Columbia, Canada

There cannot be life without air, food, and water, and we are poisoning all three. A pelican, its feathers covered in oil from the recent oil spill in the Gulf of Mexico, tries to rise out of the polluted waters, crying out to us his warning of the future we are allowing to happen.

Behind him is a flooded small town symbolizing a way of life that is drowning through the consequences of global warming. Telephone poles stand at a slant, cars are submerged, one street sign allows traffic to go straight ahead or turn left, while the one above, a one-way sign, points right. We can only go in one direction—what future will we choose?

In the small blue-green boxes at the bottom of the tapestry are further consequences of our negligence. A hermaphroditic fish with the molecular symbol for estrogen embroidered upon it represents what we are doing to the creatures with which we share the planet, literally poisoning them with our own waste. The zebra mussels and milfoil represent the invasive species that we carry in our wake as we trample over mother earth. The bits of plastic in the last two boxes were picked up on two beaches, one on the Pacific Ocean and one on the Mediterranean. We cannot sweep the refuse of our civilization beneath the sand and pretend it does not exist: it does not go away. There are vortices of garbage in the oceans circling around the natural gyres of warm ocean currents, full of plastic, dead fish, marine mammals, snared birds, and more plastic particles that will not break down in our lifetimes nor that of our grandchildren.

—Barbara Heller on her tapestry *One Way*

Barbara Heller. *Sarah Rebecca*. Handwoven tapestry: linen warp, wool weft, commercial and handspun, mostly hand-dyed. 48 x 70" (122 x 176cm). Photo: Ted Clarke: Image This.

In the *Stonewall* series and in the *Ghost Image* tapestries which evolved from them, I try to convey the spirits in the stones. When people manipulate their environment, using materials found in nature to construct walls and dwellings, something of their essence lingers long after they have departed. I try to make manifest the echoes of lives past and times lost, the traces left behind.

Flow
(Sarah Rebecca)

I am here, my children,
Still here, forever here.
Time still flows evenly, endlessly,
Suffusing all earthly things
With a past and a future, with hope and change.
But I am here, waiting patiently outside the flow,
As I have always been
In your absence.

This is your home; I am your home,
And long after the beams and rafters
Have succumbed to the relentless flow,
This will still be your source,
The silenced headwaters of your time.

Time no longer flows through me,
Nor do my eyes follow
The passing of seasons,
The rise and fall of lives,
The motions of the spheres.

I do not feel the weight of waiting
For what will or will not ever be,
Nor view the ageless scene around me
As it drifts on the tide of aeons.
I am merely here, in everything.

I am here if ever you return,
Alone, or with reluctant children,
Or just in unbidden reveries.
And whenever you do, I am here,
Waiting to live again in memory.

I am not weary of the waiting,
Nor of the view.

—Anon

Barbara Heller. *One Way*. Handwoven tapestry: linen warp, wool weft, some handspun, plastic bits, pea netting, miscellaneous fibers. 59 x 66.5" (140 X 169cm). 2013. Photo: Ted Clarke: Image This.

Barbara Heller. *One Way* (detail).

Susan Hart Henegar

La Jolla, California, USA

Horses provide unexpected adventures in the work of tapestry and fiber artist Susan Hart Henegar. She grew up in the American Southwest, creating work from personal exploration, travel photography, and childhood memories of riding. Working in the textile mediums of tapestry, quilting, embroidery, and book arts, Susan's work focuses on the narrative. Each piece in a series, with its evocative title, adds to the evolving story, thread by thread.

With an eye for symbolism and allegory, the artist interweaves a range of implications in her stories. As in medieval tapestries, present day thought and imagery suggest layers of interpretations of the viewer's time. Abstract sketches in the lightly expressed background join the silent dialogue between viewer and subject. The story evolves and tapestry has again reflected a glimpse of history.

Susan Hart Henegar. *The Travel Series: On the Brink*. Handwoven Aubusson-style tapestry: cotton warp, wool, rayon, metallic weft. 42 x 56" (105 x 140cm).

Silvia Heyden

Durham, North Carolina, USA

Silvia Heyden is a greatly admired tapestry master in the era encompassing three generations of artists in this exhibition. Having studied color and composition in the Bauhaus tradition under Johannes Itten, she arrived at her style of tapestry design and weaving with a clear sense of "...complementary relationships between function, materials, and form, between process and result." Her results amount to a body of work with a distinctive tapestry voice reflecting intimate dialogues between her inspirations and woven realizations.

In her tapestries, one sees Silvia's personal responses to nature's harmonies and the music she plays on her violin. Indeed, musical references often appear in the titles of her tapestries and in her woven rhythms, melodic phrasings and even jazz improvisations. Heyden's tapestry music plays to audiences in museums, public spaces, and private collections in the United States, Germany, and her native Switzerland.

Today we once again have the opportunity to design tapestries directly on the loom. The prerequisite is that the weaver master the language of weaving and the loom in the same way a musician must master the instrument.
—From: *The Making of Modern Tapestry: My Journey of Discovery,* by Silvia Heyden.

Silvia Heyden. *Weavers Dance.* Handwoven high-warp linen tapestry. 47 x 34" (117.5 x 85cm).

Dirk Holger

Olney, Maryland, USA

All art is based on a skillfully employed craft. The main difference between a painting and a tapestry is how the masterwork is executed.
— Dirk Holger

Dirk Holger trained at the Aubusson Tapestry School in France with artist Jean Lurçat, noted for his role in the revival of modern tapestry. In 2006 Holger curated *Tapestries: The Great Twentieth Century Modernists,* an exhibition organized for the Trust for Museum Exhibitions with works designed by twentieth century artists such as Georges Braque, Alexander Calder, Marc Chagall, Vassily Kandinsky, Henri Matisse, and Pablo Picasso. In this exhibition, which earned him the nickname "modern-day missionary for tapestry," Holger presented stunning examples of the revival period of tapestries designed by the modern masters.

Large-scale tapestries designed by artists have indeed found their way into public spaces and museums along with artist/weaver-designed smaller works created as one-of-a-kind. Returning to Holger's assertion that "All art is based on a skillfully employed craft," he shows in this exhibition one of his smaller, more personal artworks *Pour Sarah* (*For Sarah*). His own tapestry inspirations are woven mostly in Aubusson and other workshops.

Dirk Holger. *Pour Sarah* (*For Sarah*). Handwoven Aubusson tapestry. 56 x 62" (140 x 155cm).

Peter Horn

Kiel, Germany

A tapestry artist for many years, Peter Horn has exhibited his powerful handwoven expressions in solo and group exhibitions throughout eastern and western Europe, Scandinavia, Canada, Japan, and the United States.

Easter Island, an ancient, crumbling civilization that once must have been colossal and impressive, in front of a glowing red background—the glow of fire? The end of a world? Intensified by the flame-like shapes in front of disintegrating statues—which themselves are again intensified through the clash with the evenness of the parallel stripes placed underneath. This ancient civilization: still present in the realist detail, in those eyes? From the center, an almost imploring look fixates the viewer; on the right, rock formations reminiscent of monumental sculpture. Associations are evoked by forms, by colors, by their arrangement within the picture plane.

—Art Critic Karl Uphues, translation by Volker Rosenberg. Quoted from Karl Uphues essay: "Peter Horn's tapestries between 1983 and 1993," from Peter Horn's tapestry catalogue resonné: *Welt Bilder. Bild Welten (World View. View World): Werkkatalog Der Bildwebereien Von Peter Horn*.

Peter Horn. *Osterinsel (Easter Island)*. Handwoven tapestry. 32 x 26" (80 x 65cm).

Peter Horn. *Osterinsel (Easter Island) detail.*

Constance Hunt

Vallejo, California, USA

Water from the *Sketchbook Series* is one of four tapestries, each representing one of the four elements: Earth, Air, Fire, and Water. Each tapestry contains diagrams from the book *Sensitive Chaos* by Theodore Shwenk with its theory of the spiral/vortex form repeating in all forms of life. So permission was granted to include diagrams pertaining to each of the elements included in the tapestry. All of life is connected, variations of the basic spiral forms. In all of life, all the elements contain these variations of the spiral/vortex. Objects of one world emerge to be claimed by another.

>Pass by pass, image
>Creates structure: tapestry:
>An integrity.

I cannot remember a time when I did not draw or work with thread and fabric, learning many techniques. Yet, I felt the need for a stronger medium to hold larger images, ideas. It was not until a series of events unfolded that I found tapestry, or tapestry found me.

One morning, while conserving tapestry at San Francisco's DeYoung Museum's Conservation Lab, I saw through the magnifying glass two children rolling a hoop. Such detail, line, movement created on a grid fascinated me. I attended a presentation by Mark Adams, a San Francisco tapestry designer, on his work and process. I was enchanted. Members of the newly formed San Francisco Tapestry Workshop sat behind me and one invited me to attend. The San Francisco Tapestry Workshop was four blocks from where I lived. The journey into this exacting, ancient art form began and continues to challenge and enchant…tapestry…in my Constant Hunt.

—Constant Hunt.

Constance Hunt. *Water* from the *Sketchbook Series*. Handwoven tapestry 13 portée: wool weft, cotton warp. 4 x 5' (150cm).

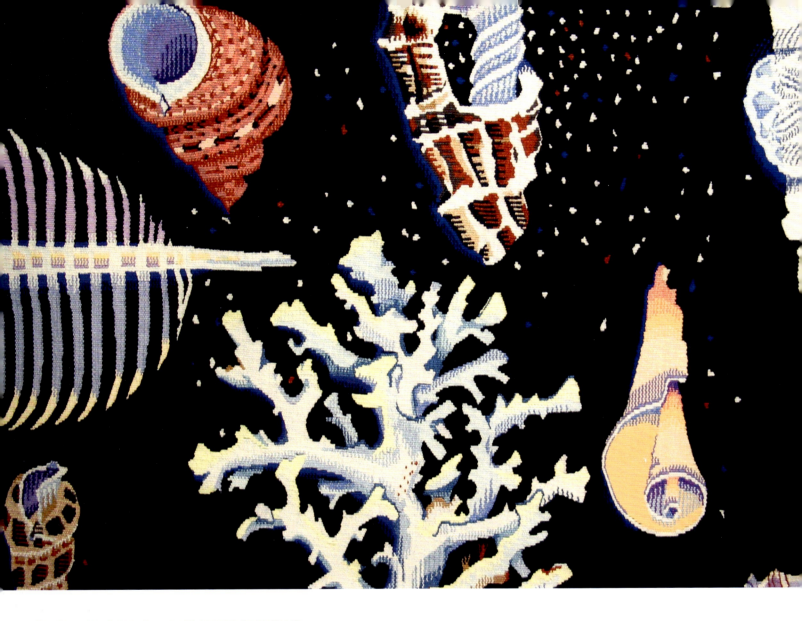

Constance Hunt. *Water* from the *Sketchbook Series* (detail).

Susan Iverson

Richmond, Virginia, USA

Susan Iverson is a professor in the School of the Arts at Virginia Commonwealth University. Her work has been exhibited widely and is included in many collections including the American Consulate in Osaka, Japan, and the Renwick Gallery of the Smithsonian American Art Museum in Washington, D.C.

My tapestries from the *Dream* series are about memories and dreams; they deal with the past and the future—both real and imagined. The sense of place and my attachment to my environment are aspects of this work. I am influenced by both the physical landscape around me and the remembered landscapes that haunt me.

Many of the tapestries include silhouettes of anonymous figures surrounded by their dreams or by a landscape that merges with them. The compositions contain multiple horizon lines. These distant lines between land and sky or water and sky may never be reached but they can provoke thoughts of another time or place.

I am intrigued with the object quality of tapestries; the density of structure and color, visual and physical textures, and the ability of tapestries to become three-dimensional through manipulation or presentation.

—Susan Iverson

Susan Iverson. *Dream Sequence.* Handwoven tapestry: wool, linen, and silk on linen warp. 32" x 6' 7.5" (80 x 79.5cm); Photo: Taylor Dabney.

Ruth Jones

Vancouver, British Columbia, Canada

Weaving by its nature is an intimate journey through the soul of an image, which has been for me a very compelling reason to pursue the art. Tapestry allows me a chance not only to order an image by pixels of hue and tonal value, but to slip into it. The extreme tactile intimacy of the process, in which I am embraced by the loom and have my hands inside the image, may account for the mysterious resonance that emanates from finished work. I initially noticed it in the works of historical and contemporary tapestries by other weavers, and was amazed to discover it, when I first began weaving, coming from my own work. I think that this fascinating emanation has fueled my commitment to a handwoven medium.

—Ruth Jones

Ruth Jones. *Woad Deva.* Handwoven tapestry: wool weft, cotton warp. 12 x 16" (30 x 40cm).

Ruth Jones. *Jardin de Pallas.* Handwoven tapestry: silk and wool weft, cotton warp. 50 x 60" (125 x 150cm).

Aino Kajaniemi

Jyväskylä, Finland

One of many honors and commissions in Aino Kajaniemi's career was Finnish Textile Artist of the Year 2010. The following year she was awarded the Golden Medal from ORNAMO, the Finnish Association of Designers, and a five-year grant from the state of Finland.

> My textiles are my way of thinking. I want to produce the objects of my wonderings into something concrete, so that I could understand them. I think about problems of the everyday life and then visualize them intricately. The subjects of my works usually originate from the inmost of a human being: sorrow, joy, uncertainty, guilt, tenderness, and memories.
>
> Very often in my tapestries I use textile as a symbol: laces, pleats, dresses, collars, socks, shoes, gloves, belt, hat, scarf, et cetera. All these are personal, intimate things which consist of similar and common memories. This symbol picture language is like international communicating without words. I build a balance of contrasts, even disagreements; a stopped moment in a picture and the achievement which takes a lot of time.
>
> In my works I use an old, troublesome technique which is hidden under simple forms and sketch-like outcomes. In a way this resembles ballet where the dance seems easy and light as a feather but in reality is lead heavy.
>
> —Aino Kajaniemi

Aino Kajaniemi. *Sounder.* Handwoven tapestry with the traditional French technique using various materials. 56.25 x 220.25" (143 x 560cm).

Jane Kidd

Salt Spring Island, British Columbia, Canada

Throughout my career as an artist I have explored ideas that reference my experience of the world. To do this I have chosen to work almost exclusively with the process of woven tapestry. I find tapestry to be a compelling medium partially because it provides a means to develop content through imagery. I am also drawn to the material identity of tapestry and I am committed to finding meaning and relevance in the process of handwork.

Within my practice I employ handwork as a human-centered activity that embraces risk and invention to create the potential for originality. I value skillful making and disciplinarily knowledge as a link to history and the tradition of makers. I see the labor-intensive nature of my process as an embodiment of time that creates a metaphoric reference to the accumulated weight of experience and history and provides a counterpoint to the temporal nature of contemporary society. I am willing to invest in hand processes as a way to pay attention and focus on the issues that I care about.

My recent works reflect the complications and contradictions of the issues we live with. The narrative ideas woven through both *Possession Series* and *Land Sentence Series* explore my interest in human/nature relationships.

In the *Possession Series* I am interested in the human desire to possess and assimilate the natural world into material culture and to recreate nature under human control through the translation of nature into the decorative systems of notation and collections. I use a compartmentalized composition to collect and juxtaposition images of historic and contemporary tools, reference to botanical drawings, diagrams, mapping, and historic textiles.

In the *Land Sentence Series* I have chosen to work largely from images that documented the changing environment collected from aerial and satellite photography and technological data. This scientific imagery can provide a beautiful yet unnerving view of our complex and often destructive relationship to the world around us. I am aware that these images represent knowledge but I am also aware that through this disorienting and disembodied technological viewpoint I can become removed and disassociated from the reality of my surroundings, failing to perceive my environment with the same sense of personal responsibility.

Jane Kidd. *Possession Series: Imprint/Impact #1.* Handwoven tapestry: wool, rayon, cotton. 53 x 24.5 " (135 x 63cm) 2004. Photo: John Dean Photography.

Jane Kidd. *Possession Series: Imprint/Impact #3*. Handwoven tapestry: wool, rayon, cotton. 54 x 24.75" (137 x 62cm) 2005. Photo: John Dean Photography.

Jane Kidd. *Possession Series: Imprint/Impact #4*. Handwoven tapestry: wool, rayon, cotton. 53 x 24.5" (135 x 63cm) 2008. Photo: John Dean Photography.

Land Sentence Series is my attempt to take a scientific worldview and, through the physicality and sensual nature of handwork, draw it back into the realm of the personal. Using the flawed and imperfect language of tapestry and the slow and intimate process of weaving, I am attempting to reinterpret and rewrite the dispassionate certainty of these technological sources and mediate recognition of the inimitable nature of our environment.

Ultimately, I hope that my tapestries will be seen as objects of expressive and sensual beauty that celebrate the handmade and encourage reflection on the world we live in.

—Jane Kidd

Jane Kidd. *Land Sentence: Pool*. Handwoven tapestry: wool, rayon, cotton. 35.75 x 81.5" (91 x 207 cm). 2010. Photo: John Dean Photography.

Lialia Kuchma

Chicago, Illinois, USA

Luke 1 connects the opening chapter from Genesis in the Old Testament, "The Spirit of God moved over the face of the deep," with Luke 1:35 from the New Testament, "And the angel answered and said to her, The Holy Ghost shall come onto you, and the power of the Highest shall overshadow you: therefore also that holy thing which shall be born of you shall be called the Son of God." The word "overshadow" conjures an image of the Spirit of God moving upon the face of the waters or "covered with the spirit of prophecy." Mary's reply to the angel in Luke 1:38, "I am the Lord's servant," may be construed as the language of faith and humble admiration, and not of confirmation. The bold, black lines symbolize the Holy Spirit in the announcement of the hypostasis of Christ, with land and waters beneath.

—Lialia Kuchma

Lialia Kuchma. *Luke I*. Handwoven tapestry: wool and cotton. 96 x 96" (165 x 165cm).

Christine Laffer

San Jose, California, USA

Having explored tapestry as a medium for many years, I have found that its physical qualities work best for me as shallow sculpture than as a flat pictorial field. These dimensional pieces use references to garments and torsos in combination, and to bodily substances that thread can represent. Their surfaces undulate and ripple from the controlled internal stresses of the weave, its eccentricities and improprieties. This type of tapestry exists outside the cultural frame established by historical tapestry and relies on its own physical presence—its texture, weight, construction methods, and way of maturing over time. Working with this physicality and the unruliness of bas-relief tapestry, I can play between the illusion of an image and the actuality of the object.

With *Signs of a Shift* I conflate female figure and evening dress which, through material and surface, represents the body/skin/garment that is both a person and a tapestry. This form incorporates several ideas: the body marked by changes or shifts in its structure, the body revealed by a second skin (the textile), and the animation the transient human occupant gives over or leaves behind in the cloth.

—Christine Laffer

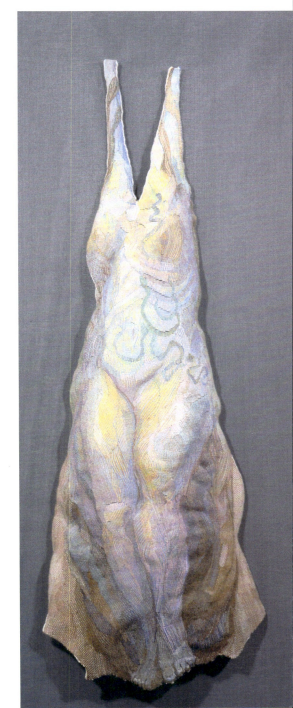

Christine Laffer.
Signs of a Shift.
Handwoven
bas-relief tapestry:
linen, wool, cotton,
silk. 56.5 x 22 x 5"
(140 x 55 x 2cm).

Ewa Latkowska-Żychska

Warsaw and Łódź, Poland

Professor Ewa Latkowska-Żychska holds a degree from the Fine Arts Academy Wladyslawa Strzeminskiego in Łódź, Poland, where she has been director of the paper-textile studio since 1997. She has exhibited her work at the Cheongju International Crafts Biennale, South Korea; Nemzetkozi Miniaturtextil—4th Triennial Of Textil Art in Szombathely, Hungary; VI Bienal Internacional de Arte Textil Contemporaneo WTA, Xalapa, Veracruz, Mexico; and the 6th and 7th International Fiberarts Biennale *From Lausanne to Beijing*, Beijing, China. Her works are in the collections of Central Museum of Textiles, Łódź, Poland; Savaria Museum, Szombathey, Hungary; and the Centrum voor Kunst en Cultuur (Center for Art and Culture), Ghent, Belgium.

I have always strived to master the skills that subjugated the tactile art materials to my will and, on the other hand, let intuition play its part—just as in nature. I wanted to narrate a textile story about my recurring inspirations: the nature of water, sky, wind, dawn, and twilight—the ordinary and extraordinary world. I have searched and searched for synthetic forms that would complement the story. The expression was always painterly in character. For every item I worked out a special weaving technique to render my intention in the best possible way. These techniques are the distinguishing feature of my wall hangings. They represent me at the world textile art exhibitions.

Creativity, which is the way to art, is the core of my life. I cannot imagine my life without creation, without my family as co-coordinators of my world. Every week I depart from Warsaw, the city where I live with my family. Landscapes mark my travel. Halfway between Łódź and Warsaw lies Bełchów. I have a patch of meadow and a hundred birches there, which grow around my cottage. I am planning to spend more time observing landscape from one viewpoint.

Dream
Images reflected from the confines of the universe
glance back in a dream
flow over tree-tops, mountain peaks and house roofs,
and awakened thoughts
piece them all
in tissue of existence.
—Ewa Latkowska-Żychska, translated by Agnieszka Grochulska

Ewa Latkowska-Żychska. *Dark Blue.* Handwoven tapestry: mixed technique, wool on linen warp. 83.5 x 80" (208 x 200 cm). Photo: Peter Mastalerz.

Bojana H. Leznicki

Verona, New Jersey, USA

Bojana Leznicki was born in Bulgaria to professional parents who fostered their daughter's free, creative spirit along with the values of love, loyalty, friendship, and hard work. Encouraged toward languages and cultures, Bojana was set for a life of rich experiences. At the Art Academy in Łódź, Poland, she joined an esteemed community of creative people. There she discovered the slow, meditative actions of weaving, which became for her a beautiful, quiet process of continuous self-discovery.

The birth of children brought delightful interruptions along with new inspirations and necessarily smaller formats for her weavings. A move to New Jersey brought dramatic change, yet reinforced her parents' values of tolerance and warmth toward all people. Overwhelmed at times by the culture of material accumulation and waste in her new country, she sought spiritual freedom and a deeper closeness to nature. Unburdening the planet and her spirit, Bojana recycled wool and other elements from her earlier art works into new tapestries created in her present place and time.

A Long Journey Starts With a First Step

I am not attached to my work and don't feel sad when old work gets recycled. I create from an inner need and cannot say what my next step will be in my artistic expression. Who knows, maybe an installation, maybe one single photograph? Step by step, one after the other, the journey of life. All it takes is to keep walking.

—Bojana Leznicki

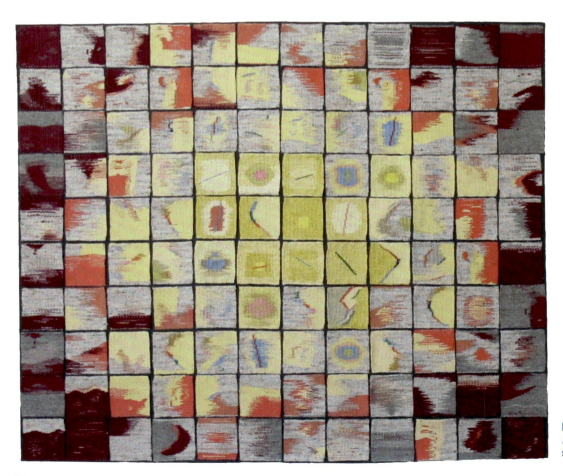

Bojana H. Leznicki. *My Little Prayer Rug*. Handwoven tapestry: wool and silk. 40 x 46" (100 x 115cm).

Lore Kadden Lindenfeld (1921-2010)

Princeton, New Jersey, USA

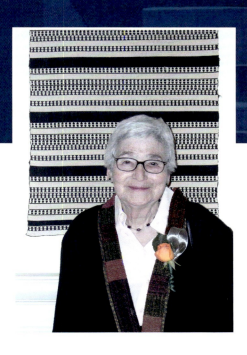

Lore Kadden Lindenfeld came to the United States as Lore Kadden in 1939 from her native Germany. Her artistic life was shaped by her years at Black Mountain College (near Asheville, North Carolina) where she became a student of Anni Albers, and so a grandchild of the Bauhaus, where Anni and her husband, Josef, had been influential members. That tradition remained a strong influence throughout Lore's life as a weaver and textile artist.

After time off to raise her children she became an instructor at Middlesex County College, where she initiated a weaving workshop. She also began to make woven wall hangings, which were widely exhibited. The Bauhaus heritage can be seen in the one illustrated here.

She approached each piece as new and rarely repeated herself. As a result her output was small and recognition came slowly. Her work is represented, among others, at the Museum of Art and Design (formerly the American Craft Museum) in New York, the Newark Museum, and in private collections. After her death in 2010, a substantial collection of her work was given to the Asheville Art Museum. Examples and biographical material may be seen at Black Mountain College Project.

— Peter Lindenfeld

Lore Lindenfeld. *Totem #2.*
Handwoven tapestry: wool warp and weft. 32 x 9" (80 x 22cm).

Yael Lurie & Jean Pierre Larochette

Berkeley, California; and Puerto Vallarta, Mexico

Yael Lurie and Jean Pierre Larochette: designer, tapestry weaver and partners in life have exhibited their collaborative works across three continents for more than four decades. Permanent homes for their tapestries exist in museums, temples and private collections throughout those continents. They have studied and taught aspects of tapestry design and technique in France, Argentina, Israel, Mexico, and the United States.

Daughter of artist Jacob Lurie, Yael studied painting with her father and also with Jacob Wexler in her native Israel. Eventually she studied tapestry weaving there with her husband, Jean Pierre. Jean Pierre Larochette studied tapestry design and weaving with his father at the Atelier Armand Larochette in Argentina where French tapestry traditions were sustained. In Israel, he studied and wove under the direction of legendary tapestry artist Jean Lurçat. He co-founded the San Francisco Tapestry Workshop, which trained and influenced a generation of tapestry artists in the United States.

Yael and Jean Pierre are true masters of the art of tapestry from inspiration to realization. Widely exhibited, collected, and admired in international fine art circles, they continue to expand their following of devoted students. Quite proudly, tapestry artists they have touched along the way show their own woven inspirations in this exhibition. Yael and Jean Pierre have thus infused the international tapestry movement with the richness of their historical and aesthetic values.

Yael Lurie and **Jean Pierre Larochette.**
Watershed. Handwoven tapestry: wool, silk, linen, metallic, and synthetic gold and cotton on cotton warp. 63 x 27" (150 x 67.5cm).
Photo: Michael Irwin.

Luis Lazo

Oaxaca, Mexico

Luis Lazo studied in his Mexican homeland with tapestry masters Yael Lurie and Jean Pierre Larochette. His tapestry *Referente Huipil #9*, a collaborative effort by Yael and Luis, refers symbolically to traditional Mexican patterns.

Luis has exhibited his tapestries at the Museo de Arte Peter Gray, Puerto Vallarta, Museo Textil de Oaxaca, the Craft Institute of Oaxaca and the Museum of Monte Alban, Oaxaca.

Yael Lurie with **Luis Lazo.** *Referente Huipil #9.*
Handwoven tapestry: wool on cotton. 26 x 17.5"
(65 x 43cm). Photo: Yadin Larochette.

Susan Martin Maffei

New Baltimore, New York, USA

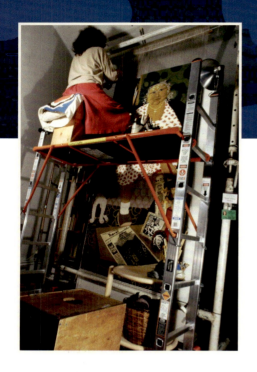

Susan Martin Maffei is an internationally known tapestry artist whose background includes studies at The Art Students League in NYC, tapestry training at Les Gobelins in Paris, and as conservator of antique textiles with special emphasis on Andean textiles at the Artweave Gallery (now Gail Martin Gallery) NYC. She has taught, lectured, and exhibited in the United States and abroad. Her tapestries have been acquired for both public and private collections including the Lloyd Cotsen Textile Traces Collection: Museum of American Folk Art in New Mexico, and the Hawaii State Foundation for the Arts, Honolulu, Hawaii.

My works in tapestry depict a very personal graphic view of the surrounding world. The historical precedent of mark-making peculiar to tapestry is coupled with the tactile and intense flavor of modern yarns and colors. Selective memory, process, and materials combine to form this imagery, which can only exist as textile. Crocheted three-dimensional trims, quipus (a system of knotted cords used by the Incas and their predecessor societies in the Andean region to store massive amounts of information important to their culture and civilization), along with found objects, enhance the narrative visuals of many works. They are influenced by the textile forms and embellishments of the ancient cultures I have explored.
—Susan Martin Maffei

Susan Martin Maffei. *Manhattan-Taxi-Please!* Handwoven tapestry. 34 x166" (85 X 270cm + woven extensions of 2' (60cm) in all directions.

Susan Martin Maffei.
Manhattan-Taxi-Please!
Installation photo: GAGA Arts Center, Garnerville, NY.

Julia Mitchell

Martha's Vineyard, Massachusetts, USA

I have always known that I would be an artist, having grown up among artists and getting plenty of encouragement as a child. Our house was full of Japanese prints, netsuke, and textiles, and my earliest memories of these still influence my view of what is beautiful. I first learned to weave at 15 from my beloved teacher and mentor, Edith Reckendorf. From her I learned of Lascaux, of medieval art history, of sound design technique, and of the art and craft of weaving. She introduced me to the great Czech tapestry designer/weavers, the work and ideas of Anni Albers, and the Bauhaus ethic of process as related to form. These together have shaped my aesthetic and my approach to the process of making art. I try always to find the meeting place between the design and the process of building it into a tapestry. At best, the materials tell me what to do, and my job becomes simply to serve as a conduit and to execute the craft as well as I can.

My subjects are, by and large, from the natural world and concern the effects of wind, water, light, and shadow over time. I try to convey a sense of the mystery in simple things, and of the unutterable beauty that surrounds us every day, whether we live in cities or suburbs or surrounded by meadows.

You mix your palette on and in the tapestry. The results are images that can only be woven.

—Julia Mitchell

Julia Mitchell. *Clouds 1 and 2*. Handwoven tapestry: wool silk and linen. 24 x 24" (60 x 60cm) each panel.

Julia Mitchell. *Rock Triptych.* Handwoven tapestry: wool and linen. 36 x 108" (90 x 43cm).

Janet Moore

Oakland, California, USA

Water, rolling and flowing, carrying silt, pebbles, leaves, animals, fish, and birds; circumscribing the landscape; each drop, part of the whole. The journey of the river is an apt metaphor for our lives. The element of water is a substance so close to our own being that without it, we are not. Poets write about it, singers honor with liquid sound the passage and flow of water in its natural habitat. Artists paint and weave the sinuous forms as they pass through and nurture our Home. Poet Claudia Schmidt writes:

Replenish!
We go on, we go on,
Canoe under the hot sun,
The upturned paddle
guides liquid to our dry mouths.
Water within us, water surrounds us,
A great mystery, our becoming dry at all.
Replenish, replenish, all must be
Replenished!
The water within and without.
All that fills us, all that surrounds us:
The great whistling pines,
The tenacious beaver,
The ancient loon,
The rush of the young eagle's wing as it
dips low over our canoe.
Replenish!

Bill Staines, singer and songwriter, asks the water:
River, take me along
In your sunshine sing me a song,
Ever moving and winding and free
You rollin' old river
You changin' old river
Let's you and me, River,
Run down to the sea.

In my home of northern California, we are in a severe drought, while in other parts of the country, water has become an overwhelming and deadly force. It is the most vital and important element of our lives. This tapestry imagines the journey of water, and the sustenance it provides for us along the way. May the rivers always flow and the grass always grow.
— Janet Moore on *River Take Me Along* and *The Green Man*

Janet Moore. *River Take Me Along.* Handwoven tapestry: wool weft on cotton warp. Each panel: 62 x 16" (155 x 40cm).

Janet Moore. *River Take Me Along (detail)*.

Janet Moore. *The Green Man.* Handwoven tapestry: Wool weft on cotton warp, mounted on gator board and lined with muslin: 36 x 35" (90 x 87.5cm). Photo: Cindy Pavlinac, San Rafael, CA.

Janet Moore. *The Green Man (detail).*

Jon Eric Riis

Atlanta, Georgia, USA

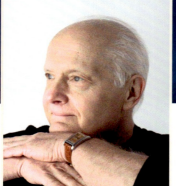

Tapestries by Jon Eric Riis captivate viewers with an unprecedented immediacy of delivery. Is it a jacket, is it three-dimensional, is it a bold political, social, or personal statement? Yes, all of that and much more. A tapestry by Riis sticks in one's mind and spirit. The significance of clothing and ornament in cultures worldwide engages a viewer at an essential level. An elegant sculptural object, handwoven in infinite detail, bears the artist's insights and stories. In the familiar and ancient voices of traditional tapestry, layers of content speak with eloquence.

At this point in his career, Riis is known worldwide for his distinctive tapestries, informed visually and intellectually by extensive research into the historical textiles of pre-Columbian Peru, Imperial China, and Russian ecclesiastical vestments. Educated at the School of the Art Institute of Chicago and Cranbrook Academy of Art, Riis followed up with a Fulbright Grant to attend Viswa Bharati University, Santiniketan, West Bengal, India.

Among the artist's many museum holdings are: the Metropolitan Museum, New York; the Art Institute of Chicago; the Museum of Art and Design, New York; the Renwick Gallery of the Smithsonian American Art Museum, Washington, D.C.; and the Atlanta Museum of Art and Design, Atlanta, Georgia.

Jon Eric Riis. *Ambush Coat*. Handwoven tapestry: freshwater pearls, turquoise, metallic thread, leather, crystals, beads. 30 x 68" (75 x 170cm). Private collection.

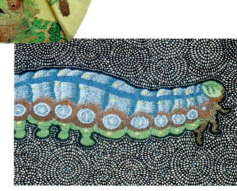

Jon Eric Riis. *Cycles II.* Handwoven tapestry: silk, leather, pearls, coral beads. 84 x 24" (210 x 60cm). Private collection.

Ramona Sakiestewa

Santa Fe, New Mexico, USA

I was born in the American Southwest. At an early age I knew I would be an artist. Having had a somewhat harried childhood, I did art-making as a way to create order out of uncertainty.

My professional art career began in tapestry weaving. That art form allowed for the blending of shapes and layering of colors. Early work was graphic in design, which eventually evolved into abstract and painterly weavings. Themes that continue to thread through my artwork are puzzle pieces, astronomical configurations, and divination. Recently I have reached back to my childhood to retrieve an early design vocabulary lexicon. These can be seen in new work called ...and Other Shapes.

—Ramona Sakiestewa

In addition to her own one-of-a-kind weavings, Ramona wove the work of Frank Lloyd Wright, Kenneth Noland, and Paul Brach. Her artwork has been widely acquired over the years. She has teamed with nationally known architects designing elements for buildings including the National Museum of the American Indian, Washington, D.C.

Selected awards and distinctions include "Gift to the Nation," Friends of Art and Preservation in Embassies, 2001; the New Mexico Governor's Award for Excellence in the Arts, 2006; the New Mexico Committee of the National Museum of Women in the Arts, and induction to the New Mexico Women's Hall of Fame 2007.

Her home and studio are in Santa Fe, New Mexico. However, travel continues to inspire her. She has lived and worked in New York City, Mexico City, Peru, Japan, China, Italy, and most recently northern Iraq.

Ramona Sakiestewa. Nebula 12. Handwoven tapestry: 36 x 35.5" (90 x 99cm).

Micala Sidore

Northampton, Massachusetts, USA

Tapestry is, at its most basic, cloth. Its manufacture has direction—you weave it from one end to the other and you cannot return to what you have woven earlier without eliminating everything in–between. Having begun with nothing but the frame of the loom, the tapestry weaver creates the field and the objects in the field all of a piece, simultaneously.

Words, conversations, poems and literature all inspire me. I am most at ease in the realm of language. This translates into visual imagery which, at its most effective, provokes the viewer to reflect on what the tapestry tells them. Sometimes the tapestry relates a story, and sometimes the tapestry teaches something about the process of weaving.

—Micala Sidore

Micala Sidore. *Black & White & Red All Over #45 – Gdye kranya ploschad No. 2*. Handwoven tapestry: cotton weft on cotton seine twine warp. 32.5 x 22" (81 x 55cm).

Micala Sidore. *Black & White & Red All Over #27 – Names of Reds.* Handwoven tapestry: wool and cotton weft on cotton seine twine warp. 24 x 30" (60 x 75cm).

Elinor Steele

New Haven, Vermont, USA

My design process for the *Reconstruction* series involves deconstructing shapes and images until they are no longer recognizable, and then reorganizing them in a new composition that has strength and balance. At first these designs represented a metaphor for rebuilding the fragments left by an act of violence. My process of layering images through transparency and erasure has evolved to represent the paradox of viewing multiple planes at once within the composition. Scale and position may shift in order. Elements of heat and fire, molten and stratified earth, water, sky, and space are suggested through color and texture. Architecture and nature become intertwined through geometry, pattern, and reflection.
—Elinor Steele

Elinor Steele. *Reconstruction II*. Handwoven tapestry: wool weft on cotton warp. 48 x 48" (120 x 120cm).

Elinor Steele. *Reconstruction IV*. Handwoven tapestry: wool weft on cotton warp. 51 x 44.5" (127.5 x 120cm).

Sarah Swett

Moscow, Idaho, USA

Sarah Swett was born in Brooklyn, NY, moved to Idaho at the age of eighteen, and has devoted the subsequent decades to telling long, slow stories with handspun yarn. Her work travels the world in books, magazines, and exhibitions. She does her best to stay at home eating cinnamon toast and learning to play the concertina.

> The ideal project takes over my life and requires a season or two to complete. Or a year. Or three. It demands time but not money. Or new clothes. Sometimes it is new clothes.
>
> —Sarah Swett

Thus is the life of many tapestry artists, though Sarah Swett's tapestries deliver a rare spontaneity of imagery through her slow process of realization. So must a viewer take time to engage fully with all possibilities in her woven observations. The titles of her tapestry series entice, yet allow for the viewer's own perspective. Two examples of this are *Casting Off,* a story through time, and *Rough Copy,* handwoven pages from an unpublished manuscript.

In a manner similar to her process, Sarah's tapestries require a quiet moment and an open mind to fully unravel. At first a viewer senses unresolved tension among an overview of familiar things. Seduced then into Sarah's compelling settings, we engage with her stories and recognize bits of our own, wishing we had thought of it in that very way. Throughout, we appreciate the wonder of handspun, handwoven threads and their supporting role in the dramas.

Sarah C. Swett.
Hang Up and Draw.
Handwoven tapestry:
wool warp and weft;
natural dye. 56 x 37"
(140 x 92.5cm). 2008.
Photo: Mark LaMoreaux.

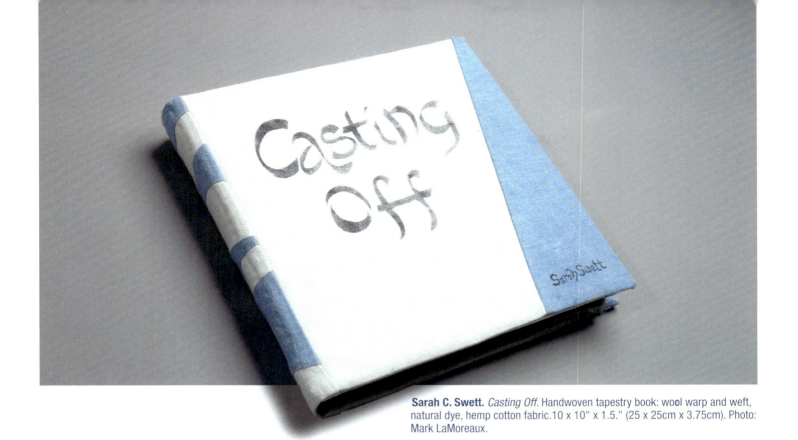

Sarah C. Swett. *Casting Off.* Handwoven tapestry book: wool warp and weft, natural dye, hemp cotton fabric. 10 x 10" x 1.5." (25 x 25cm x 3.75cm). Photo: Mark LaMoreaux.

Sarah C. Swett. *Casting Off* (inside pages view #1).

Sarah C. Swett. *Casting Off* (inside pages view #2).

Sarah C. Swett. *Casting Off* (inside pages view #3).

Sarah C. Swett. *Casting Off* (inside pages view #4).

Linda Wallace

Nanoose Bay, British Columbia, Canada

Scientific knowledge is expanding exponentially while I create art in a medium steeped in time. Working alone at the loom, weaving symbolic imagery line by line, the process promotes additional connections of time, labor, and thought. The hand of the artist is evident and unavoidable. Cloth carries signifiers of home and comfort and is used cross-culturally to visually create symbolic importance at life's passages: birth, puberty, marriage, death. Cloth is used to denote individuality or membership in a societal group. Tapestry carries European historical connections to worlds of power and influence. These voices add to the chorus of whispered dialogue.

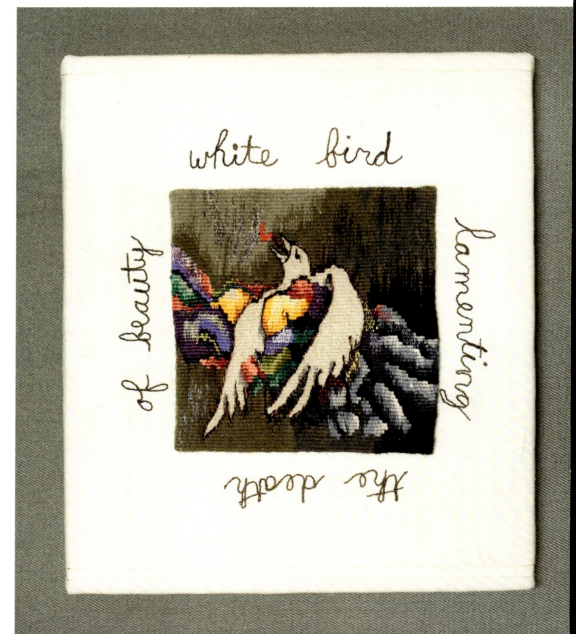

Linda M. Wallace. *Hanging by a thread.* Handwoven tapestry and hand stitching: wool, linen, cotton, rayon chenille, metallic on cotton seine twine warp. Additional materials: pink satin ribbon, linen and cotton backing. 22 x 16 x 1.5" (55 x 40 x 3.75cm). Photo: Terry Zlot.

The more I know, the more I read, the more worried I become. Despite this worry, I am also intrigued, excited, and fascinated. Immortality is being discussed by apparently rational scientists. If we are not predestined to age and die, will fertility still matter? If women's bodies are no longer necessary for the gestation of new life, what value will women have in traditional, patriarchal societies? Will those lining up to participate in genetic enhancement or blending human with machine continue to extend compassion to those dying of malnutrition, malaria, HIV? What of war, aggression, the market economy in this new chimerical world?

Feminist and artist. Filled with questions, worry, and hope.

—Linda Wallace

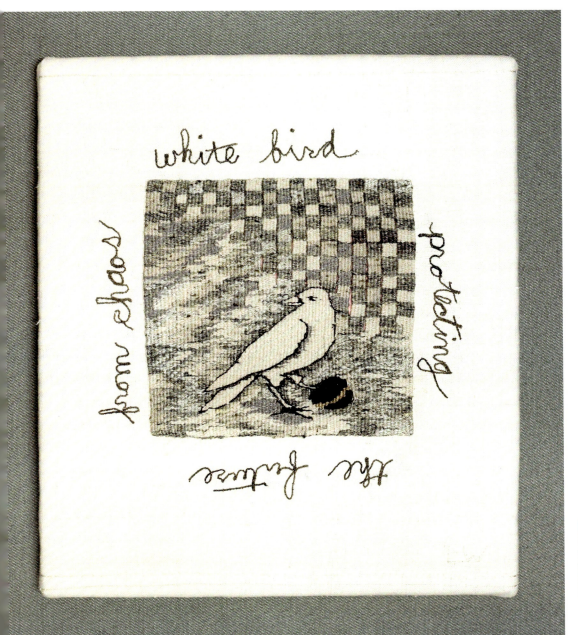

Linda M. Wallace. *Threadbare.* Handwoven tapestry and hand stitching: wool, linen, silk, cotton, metallic on cotton seine twine warp. Backing: linen and cotton. 22 x 16 x 1.5" (55 x 40 x 3.75cm). Photo: Terry Zlot.

Seven days in, she carved off her braids, slicing precisely through each wayward strand till the last hank severed and a pair of plaits fell into her hand.

"There's not much to eat," she said to the mule. "And we're absolutely lost, but I've heard a new hairdo fixes everything." And coiling eleven years around a stob, she pinned each with a thorn.

A tear welled as she turned away. She dashed it to the ground. An itch took its place and she scrubbed with a knuckle. But the more she scratched, the pricklier it grew. She frisked her scalp—it jumped to her neck. She scraped her shoulders—it crept down her spine. She wrenched off jacket, pants, chemise, whipped belly and breasts with her bra, clawed invisible hair from the backs of her knees until, undone, she hurled herself into the creek where an eddy of snowmelt jolted her into repose.

"So what do you th-think," she asked the mule. "Is it me?"

Sarah C. Swett. *Rough Copy 4: Receipt.* Handwoven tapestry: wool warp and weft, natural dye. 82 x 24 (205 x 60cm). Photo: Mark LaMoreaux.

Glossary

Aubusson: A French tapestry workshop, originally located in the region of central France known as La Marche. The term also refers to tapestries woven on low-warp looms with treadles.

Batten: The beater on a floor or table loom; also, a flat, smooth, sword-shaped stick used to hold open the shed on a tapestry loom.

Beat: To pack weft yarn into a shed.

Beauvais tapestry: Any product of the tapestry factory established in 1664 in Beauvais, France, by two Flemish weavers, Louis Hinart and Philippe Behagle. Although it was under the patronage of Jean-Baptiste Colbert, the finance minister to Louis XIV, and was subsidized by the state, the Beauvais works was a private enterprise second in importance after the Gobelins. During the French Revolution, the workshops were temporarily closed following a dispute between the weavers and the administration, and then were reopened, under state direction, making little but upholstery covers.

Block: To set the weave of a tapestry with a careful application of moisture followed by a slow drying process.

Cartoon: A tapestry design painted or drawn to full scale.

Comb: A fork-shaped hand tool used by tapestry artists for packing wefts.

Complete pass: In tapestry weaving, the term complete pass refers to the covering of every warp on both sides of the textile with weft yarn. Therefore, two half passes (two rows or picks of weaving) cover the warps on both the front and back of a tapestry. The first half pass covers alternate warps as it travels in one direction; the second half pass covers the opposite alternate warps as it travels in the opposite direction.

Concept: The idea within a design as expressed by its visual elements.

Design: The fully resolved plan for a textile or tapestry including its format, organization, proportions, color relationships, etc.

Edging cord: Plied cords caught in the selvedges of a Navajo tapestry for additional strength and reinforcement.

E.P.I.: Ends (warps) per inch; refers to the sett of the warp.

Fiber: The material from which yarn is spun.

Finishing: The process of blocking and hemming a tapestry after it has been removed from the loom.

Frame loom: The simplest type of loom. Its only function is to hold warps taut and parallel. The weaver's hands perform all other tasks.

Gobelin: The French tapestry workshop *Manufacture Nationale des Gobelins*, still in operation as a state-run institution with 30 staff members and 15 looms. Each year there are six to seven pieces that "fall from the loom." Gobelin is also a term used to describe traditional flat-woven tapestry or interlocking wefts. A Gobelin-style loom would be a vertical tapestry loom with roller beams and a simple hand-manipulated system for opening the two sheds.

Hachures: (noun, plural) In this text, hachures are triangular interpenetrations of contrasting weft colors. See Hatch and Hatchings.

Half pass: A single pick or row of weaving. Tapestry requires two half passes (one complete pass) to cover completely all warps on both the front and the back of the textile.

Hatch: (verb) To create interpenetrating lines or triangles of contrasting weft colors.

Hatchings: (noun, plural) Similar to hachures, often used to describe a less formal style of interpenetrating weft colors.

Heading: Several tightly woven passes of plain weave at the beginning and end of a tapestry.

Heddle: A wire or string with an eye through which a warp thread passes. The heddles on a loom physically position the warps for an open shed.

Hem: The heading on a tapestry turned back as a finished edge.

High-warp: A tapestry loom on which the warp yarns are stretched vertically.

Interlace: To interweave weft yarns with a warp to make cloth.

Interlock: To cross adjacent wefts between warps; also a noun referring to the crossed wefts.

Kilim: A weft-face, flat-woven rug or other textile, completely reversible, involving the slit tapestry technique.

Lazy line: A subtle, textural line traveling through the background of certain tapestries and Navajo rugs. A lazy line is created by a diagonal pattern of relays executed by two wefts of the same color.

Manufacture des Gobelins: The Manufacture des Gobelins is a tapestry factory in Paris, France, at 42 avenue des Gobelins, near the Les Gobelins métro station. It is best known as a royal factory supplying the court of Louis XIV and later monarchs; it is now run by the French Ministry of Culture, open for guided tours several afternoons per week by appointment.

Maquette: A small-scale design.

Navajo tapestry: Flat-woven, weft-face wool rugs, blankets, or tapestries all of which are seldom considered these days in useful terms. Rather they are highly prized works of art most likely to be displayed as fine art. The design of a traditional Navajo rug is usually balanced and geometric, with simple color organization. The cultural distinction of a Navajo weaving is its continuous warp resulting in four selvedges.

Pick: A single passage of the bobbin or butterfly carrying the weft through a shed. The same meanings as a row, a shot, or a half pass.

Pick-and-pick: A technique for weaving contrasting colors of weft into the two opposite tapestry sheds, resulting in narrow vertical stripes.

Plain weave: A weave structure in which the weft passes over odd numbered warps in one shed and even numbered warps in the alternate shed. Plain weave and tabby are woven in a manner similar to tapestry, though a weft-face structure is implicit in tapestry.

Ply: To twist together two or more spun yarns for additional strength.

Pointillism: The technique of painting or weaving tiny dots of colors, contrasting in hue and temperature though not intended by the artist to be perceived individually. From a distance, pointillist dots interact to become shimmering new colors in the eyes and mind of the viewer.

Portée: A portée is 12 warp ends. The density of a tapestry's warp is defined by the number of portée in a 16-inch (40-cm) section.

P.P.I.: Picks per inch. Refers to the number of weft passes per inch of weaving.

Relay: The actions of tapestry wefts as they travel toward one another, then reverse direction.

Rölakan: Swedish or Norwegian method for interlocking adjacent wefts.

Selvedge: The outside edge of a textile. The term implies a *woven* rather than a *raw* or *cut* edge.

Selvedge warps: The two warps at the extreme right and left edges of the weaving.

Sett: The number of warp threads per inch. For example, a sett of six implies a cloth woven with six warp threads per inch.

Shed: An opening created by raising alternate warps, allowing weft to pass through horizontally to form a woven cloth.

Shot: One row of weaving; the same as one pick or one half pass.

Shuttle: A shuttle holds a supply of weft yarn and carries it through a shed. Craftspeople have invented various types of shuttles for specific weaving purposes. Tapestry artists frequently prefer the simplest shuttle of all—a butterfly.

Singles: Yarn that is not plied.

Slit: A pair of adjacent interior selvedges in the woven structure of a tapestry or rug caused by relaying adjacent wefts around the same two warps several passes in succession.

Soumak: An ancient technique for knotting wefts around warps to produce a dense, evenly textured textile.

Tapestry beater: Comb.

Tapestry bobbin: A bobbin used to hold a small supply of weft yarn for tapestry weaving. Tapestry bobbins may have rounded or pointed ends.

Tapestry loom: A vertical or high-warp loom. It may be designed to sit on the floor, a table, or a lap.

Tapestry weaving: The interweaving of individual, discontinuous weft yarns with tensioned warp yarns, through two alternate sheds, resulting in a weft-surface textile constructed simultaneously with its patterns or images.

Textile: A woven, knitted, crocheted, felted, pieced, or embellished cloth. Into this category would fall rugs, tapestries, garments, household linens, and fabrics.

Texture: The surface quality of an object or the illusion thereof.

Twining: A method of wrapping pairs of wefts around the warps: may be used as a warp spacer on a tapestry loom.

Value: The relative lightness or darkness of a color.

Warp: The threads stretched vertically on a loom.

Warp-face: A woven structure characterized by a dominant proportion of warp, resulting in a textile in which the weft is covered on both sides by a densely sett warp.

Weaving: Interlacing horizontal weft threads with vertical warp threads to make a cloth.

Web: The woven cloth.

Weft: The horizontal threads interlacing with the warp.

Weft crossing: Refers to the secure joining of adjacent wefts either around a common warp or in a space between two warps.

Weft-face: A woven structure characterized by a dominant proportion of weft, resulting in a dense, heavy textile with its warps covered front and back.

Weft tail: The cut end of a tapestry weft, which must be secured in some manner.

Woof: Synonym for weft, no longer commonly used.

> There was nothing
> to fill her belly in
> the days after that
> but things the mule
> ate first--green stuff
> she hoped was
> miner's lettuce,
> and wizened elder-
> berries; and water.
> But by then she was
> too faded to care.

Sarah C. Swett. *Rough Copy 5: There was nothing.* Handwoven tapestry: wool warp and weft, natural dye. 40 x 30" (100 x 75cm). Photo: Mark LaMoreaux.

Bibliography

Adelson, C. *European Tapestry in the Minneapolis Institute of Arts*. Minneapolis, MN: Institute, 1994.

Albers, Anni. *On Weaving*. Middletown, CT: Wesleyan UP, 1965.

Amsden, Charles Avery. *Navaho Weaving, Its Technique and History*. Glorieta, NM: Rio Grande, 1972.

Auther, Elissa. *String, Felt, Thread: The Hierarchy of Art and Craft in American Art*. Minneapolis: University of Minnesota, 2010.

Autour Des "Fructus Belli". *Une Tapisserie De Bruxelles Du XVIe Siècle: Musée National De La Renaissance, Château D'Ecouen*. Paris: Réunion Des Musées Nationaux, 1992.

Baizerman, Suzanne, and Ramona Sakiestewa. *Ramona Sakiestewa: Patterned Dreams: Textiles of the Southwest*. Santa Fe: Wheelwright Museum of the American Indian, 1989.

Bennett, Anna G. *Five Centuries of Tapestry from the Fine Arts Museums of San Francisco*. San Francisco: Fine Arts Museums of San Francisco, 1992.

Biryukova, N. Ju. *The Hermitage, Leningrad: Gothic and Renaissance Tapestries*. London: Paul Hamlyn, 1965.

Black Mountain College Project. http://blackmountaincollegeproject.org

Blazkova, Jarmila. *Tapiserie XVI - XVIII Stoleti: V Umeleckoprumyslovém Muzeu v Praze*. Praha: Umeleckoprumyslové Muzeum v Praze, 1975.

Monica, Roger G. Tanner, and Bertil Lundgren. *Design in Sweden*. Stockholm: Swedish Institute, 1985.

Campbell, Thomas P., and Bruce White. *Tapestry in the Renaissance: Art and Magnificence*. New York: Metropolitan Museum of Art, 2006.

Campbell, Thomas P. *Tapestry in the Baroque: Threads of Splendor*. New York: Metropolitan Museum of Art, 2007.

Candee, Helen Churchill. *The Tapestry Book*. UK: Tudor, 1935.

Cassou, Jean, Max Damain, and Renée Moutard-Uldry. *La Tapisserie Française Et Les Peintres Cartonniers*. Paris: Editions Tel., 1957.

Cavallo, Adolph S. *Medieval Tapestries in the Metropolitan Museum of Art*. New York: Metropolitan Museum of Art, 1993.

Cavallo, Adolph S. *The Unicorn Tapestries at the Metropolitan Museum of Art*. New York: Metropolitan Museum of Art, 1998.

Chicago, Judy, and Donald Woodman. *The Dinner Party from Creation to Preservation*. London: Merrell, 2007.

Chicago, Judy. *Holocaust Project: From Darkness into Light*. New York: Penguin, 1993.

Colchester, Chloë. *Textiles Today: A Global Survey of Trends and Traditions*. London: Thames & Hudson, 2009.

Constantine, Mildred, and Jack Lenor Larsen. *The Art Fabric: Mainstream*. New York: Van Nostrand Reinhold, 1976.

Constantine, Mildred and Jack Lenor Larsen. *Beyond Craft: The Art Fabric*. New York: Van Nostrand Reinhold, 1973.

Crockett, Candace, Mark Johnson, and Julius Lang. *The Fabric of Life: 150 Years of Northern California Fiber Art History* (exhibition catalog). San Francisco State University, Art Department Gallery. San Francisco: 1997.

Delmarcel, Guy, and Erik Duverger. *Bruges Et La Tapisserie*. Bruges: Louis De Poortere, 1987.

Dobrànyi, András. *Kárpit: Nemzetközi Millenniumi Kortárs Kiállítás*. Budapest: Szépművészeti Múzeum, 2001.

Dockstader, Frederick J. *The Song of the Loom: New Traditions in Navajo Weaving*. New York: Hudson Hills in Association with the Montclair Art Museum, 1987.

Eckhardt, F. *Exhibition of the High Art of Tapestry Weaving*. Winnipeg: Winnipeg Art Gallery. 1954.

Emőke, László ,and Enikő Körtvélyessy. *Flemish and French Tapestries in Hungary*. Budapest: Corvina Kiadó, 1981.

Erlande-Brandenburg, Alain. *La Dame À La Licorne*. Paris: Éditions De La Réunion Des Musées Nationaux, 1978.

Feder, Norman. *American Indian Art*. New York: H.N. Abrams, 1973.

Freeman, Margaret B. *The Unicorn Tapestries*. New York: Metropolitan Museum of Art, 1976.

Geijer, A. *A History of Textile Art*. Stockholm: Philip Wilson Publishers Ltd. 1979.

Gustafson, P. Tapestry: An affirmation. In B. Heller (Ed.) *Weaving between the lines: BC Tapestry on the edge*. Vancouver: BC Stars. (1997).

Hedlund, Ann Lane, Teresa Wilkins, and Diana Leonard. *Beyond the Loom: Keys to Understanding Early Southwestern Weaving*. Boulder: Johnson, 1990.

Hedlund, Ann Lane. *Navajo Weaving in the Late 20th Century: Kin, Community, and Collectors*. Tucson: University of Arizona, 2004.

Hedlund, Ann Lane. *Reflections of the Weaver's World: The Gloria F. Ross Collection of Contemporary Navajo Weaving*. Denver: Denver Art Museum, 1992.

Heller, Barbara. Collaboration through Community Tapestry. Heller (Ed.) *Weaving between the lines: BC Tapestry on the edge*. Vancouver: BC Stars. (1997).

Heyden, Silvia. *The Making of Modern Tapestry: My Journey of Discovery*. Research Triangle Park, NC: S. Heyden, 1998.

Jarry, Madeleine. *La Tapisserie: Art Du Xxème SIECLE*. Fribourg: Office Du Livre, 1974.

Jarry, Madeleine. *World Tapestry, from Its Origins to the Present*. New York: Putnam, 1969.

Jefferies, Janis. *Reinventing Textiles: Gender and Identity*: Telos, 2001.

Jepson Gallerie, Inc. and French & Company Inc. (Published Jointly by). *Murals of Wool*. Washington, DC, 1960.

Jobé, Joseph, and Pierre Verlet. *Great Tapestries; the Web of History from the 12th to the 20th Century*. Lausanne: Edita, 1965.

Jones, R. (2012): Ruth Jones: Art Tapestry. *Ruth Jones Studios*. Retrieved July 4, 2014, from http://www.ruthjones.ca

Jones, S., & Holden, J. (2008). *It's a material world: caring for the public realm*. London: Demos.

Joubert, Fabienne. *La Tapisserie Médiévale Au Musée De Cluny*. Paris: Ministère De La Culture Et De La Communication, Editions De La Réunion Des Musées Nationaux, 1987.

Kalniete, Sandra, and Mārtiņš Heimrāts. *Latvju Tekstilmāksla (Latvian Tapestry)*. Rīga: Liesma, 1989.

Kidd, J. (2012, July 14). Translations. *Alberta Craft Magazine*, 2, 4.

Koenig, Harriet, and Seymour H. *Navajo Weaving, Navajo Ways*. Katonah, NY: Katonah Gallery, 1986.

Korchounova, T.T, and I.M. Lasinskaia. *Russian Tapestry: St.Petersbourg Tapestry Factory (Russische Bildteppiche: Die Petersburger Gobelinmanufaktur. N. p.)* Khoudojnik RSFSR, 1975.

Korwin, L. *Textiles as Art: Selecting, Framing, Mounting, Lighting and Maintaining Textile Art*. Chicago: Laurence Korwin, 1990.

Koumis, Matthew. *Art Textiles of the World: Great Britain*. Brighton, UK: Telos Art, 2006.

Koumis, Matthew. *Art Textiles of the World: Japan: Volume 2*. Winchester, UK: Telos Art, 2002.

Koumis, Matthew. *Art Textiles of the World: Scandinavia, Volume 2*. Bristol, UK: Telos Art, 2005.

Koumis, Matthew. *Art Textiles of the World, USA*. Winchester, UK: Telos, 2000.

Krondahl, Hans, Mailis Stensman, Tonie Lewenhaupt, and Göran Söderlund. *Hans Krondahl: Textila Verk*. Stockholm: Carlsson I Samarbete Med Prins Eugens Waldemarsudde, 2009.

Kybalová, Ludmila. *Contemporary Tapestries from Czechoslovakia*. London: A. Wingate, 1965.

Laurence, R. Barbara Heller: Medium and Message. In *Falling from Grace: The Tapestries of Barbara Heller*. Maple Ridge Pitt Meadows Arts Council.

Lium, Randi Nygaard. *Ny Norsk Billedvev: Et Gjennombrudd*. Oslo: C. Huitfeldt, 1992.

Lurçat, Jean. *Jean Lurçat Le Chant Du Monde Angers: Musée Jean Lurçat, Ancien Hôpital Saint-jean, Angers*. Angers: Siraudeau, 1980.

Maguire, Eunice Dauterman, and Rose Choron. *Weavings from Roman, Byzantine, and Islamic Egypt: The Rich Life and the Dance*. Champaign, Illinois: Krannert Art Museum, University of Illinois at Urbana-Champaign, 1999.

Marks, R. Medieval Europe: Tapestries. In Norwich, J.J. *The Burrell Collection*. (pp. 101-109) Glasgow: William Collins Sons and Company Ltd., 1985

Mirzaghitova, Z. (2012). *The Hunt of the Unicorn interview with Ruth Jones*. http://satellitegallery.wordpress.com/2013/12/07/the-hunt-of-the-unicorn-interview-with-ruth-jones

Mayer-Thurman, Christa C. *Textiles in the Art Institute of Chicago*. Chicago: Art Institute of Chicago, 1992.

McQuiston, Don, Debra McQuiston, Lynne Bush, and Tom Till. *The Woven Spirit of the Southwest*. San Francisco: Chronicle, 1995.

Meyer, Daniel. *L'histoire Du Roy*. Paris: Editions De La Reunion Des Musees Nationaux, 1980.

Monem, Nadine Käthe. *Contemporary Textiles: The Fabric of Fine Art*. London: Black Dog, 2008.

Moorman, Theo. *Weaving as an Art Form: A Personal Statement*. West Chester, Schiffer, 1975.

Morandini, Gina, and Daniela Zanella. *Tessuti in Friuli*. Tarcento, Italy: Le Arti Tessili, 1988.

Müntz, Eugène, and Louisa J. Davis. *A Short History of Tapestry. From the Earliest times to the End of the 18th Century*. London: Cassell, 1885.

Ortiz, Antonio Domínguez, Concha Herrero Carretero, and José A Godoy. *Resplendence of the Spanish Monarchy: Renaissance Tapestries and Armor from the Patrimonio Nacional*. New York: Metropolitan Museum of Art, 1991.

Ota Memorial Museum of Art. *Ukiyo-e Masterpieces in the Collection of the Ota Memorial Museum of Art*. Tokyo: Ota Memorial Museum of Art, 1988.

Peltovuori, Sinikka. *Linnut Liiteli Sanoja: Laila Karttunen Kuvatekstilien Problematiikkaa*. Helsinki: Yliopistopaino, 1995.

Pershing, L. Peace work out of piecework: Feminist needlework metaphors and the ribbon around the Pentagon. In S. Tower Hillis, L. Pershing, & M. J. Yeung (Eds.), *Feminist theory and the study of folklore*. Chicago: University of Illinois Press, 1993.

Pershing, L. *The ribbon around the Pentagon: Peace by piecemakers*. Knoxville: The University of Tennessee Press, 1996).

Phillips, Barty. *Tapestry*. London: Phaidon, 1994.

Planchenault, René. *The Angers Tapestries*. Paris: Caisse Nationale Des Monuments Historiques Et Des Sites, 1980.

Planchenault, René, and Danis Mahaffey. *Some Notes about the Angers Tapestries*. Paris: Caisse Nationale Des Monuments Historiques Et Des Sites, 1977.

Poutasuo, Tuula. *Tekstiilin Taidetta Suomesta (Textile Art in Finland)*. Hamina, Finland: AKATIMI in Cooperation with Textile Artists in Finland TEXO Ry, 2001.

Rapp, Buri Anna, and Monica Stucky-Schurer. *Zahm Und Wild: Basler Und Strassburger Bildteppiche*. Mainz: Von Zabern, 1990.

Reichard, Gladys Amanda. *Spider Woman: A Story of Navajo Weavers and Chanters*. Glorieta, NM: Rio Grande, 1968.

Rekertaitė-Načiulienė, Daiva, and Silverija Stelingienė. *Lietuvos Gobelenas*. Vilnius: Vaga, 1983.

Russell, Carol K. *Exhibit 2, ITNET: ITNET & the Anchorage Museum of History and Art: Sponsored by Alaska State Council on the Arts*. Anchorage, AK, USA: ITNET, 1992.

Russell, Carol K. *Fiber Art Today*. Atglen, PA: Schiffer, 2011.

Russell, Carol K. *Tapestry Handbook: The Next Generation*. Atglen, PA: Schiffer, 2007.

Russell, Carol K., and Carol Westfall, Archie Brennan, Bojana H. Leznicki, Lore Lindenfeld, Susan Martin Maffei, Patricia Malarcher, Soyoo Hyunjoo Park, Joy Saville, and Betty Vera. *Visions in Fiber: Today's Textiles as Fine Art*. South Orange, NJ: Gallery of South Orange, 1997.

Salet, Francis. *David Et Bethsabée: Château D'Écouen*. Paris: Éditions De La Réunion Des Musées Nationaux. 1980.

Schneebalg-Perelman, Sophie, and Pierre Verlet. *Les Chasses De Maximilien: Les Énigmes D'un Chef-d'oeuvre De La Tapisserie*. Brussels: Les Editions De Chabassol, 1982.

Schoeser, Mary. *World Textiles: A Concise History*. London: Thames & Hudson, 2003.

Sevensma, W. S., and Alexis Brown. *Tapestries*. New York: Universe, 1965.

Sosset, Léon-Louis. *Tapisserie Contemporaine En Belgique (Hedendaagse Wandtapijten in België)*. Liège: Perron, 1989.

Souchal, Geneviève, Richard Oxby, and Francis Salet. *Masterpieces of Tapestry From the Fourteenth to the Sixteenth Century: An Exhibition at the Metropolitan Museum of Art*. Paris: Éditions Des Musées Nationaux, 1973.

Spurný, Jan, and Antonín Kybal. *Modern Textile Designer, Antonín Kybal*. Prague: Artia, 1960.

Stanfill, Silver. *Exhibit 1, ITNET: ITNET & the Anchorage Museum of History and Art*. Anchorage, AK, USA: ITNET, 1990.

Stroud, Marion Boulton, and Kelly Mitchell. *New Material as New Media: The Fabric Workshop and Museum*. Cambridge, MA: MIT, 2002.

Talley, Charles S. *Contemporary Textile Art: Scandinavia*. Carmina, 1982. Print.

Taylor, Dianne. *The First through the Tenth Biennales Internationales de la Tapisserie, Lausanne, Switzerland*, dissertation, University Microfilms International. Ann Arbor, Michigan, 1983.

Thomas, Michel, Christine Mainguy, and Sophie Pommier. *Textile Art*. Geneva: Skira, 1985.

Thomson, F. P. *Tapestry: Mirror of History*. New York: Crown, 1980.

Timmer, Dery. *Art Textiles of the World: The Netherlands*. UK: Telos Art, 2002.

Trouton, L. Peace and interconnection through public textile projects. *The Space Between* conference proceedings. Perth: Curtin University. 2004.

Trouton, L. An intimate monument: Re-narrating 'the troubles,' the Irish linen memorial, 2001-2005. Unpublished doctorate of creative arts thesis exegesis. Wollongong: University of Wollongong. 2005.

Trouton, L. Know who you are and where you come from: Debra Sparrow, Salish-Musqueam Weaver, interview. In Collett, A. (Ed.) *Kunapipi: Journal of Postcolonial Writing*, XXIII, 2 (pp. 77-93). Wollongong: University of Wollongong. 2001.

Trouton, L. From her Grandmother's House: Craftivist & Community Public Artist Interview: Bernie Williams, Haida. In Collett, A. (Ed.) *Kunapipi: Journal of Postcolonial Writing*, XXIII, 2 (pp. 63-76). Wollongong: University of Wollongong. 2001.

Victorian Tapestry Workshop. *Australian Tapestries: From the Victorian Tapestry Workshop.* South Melbourne: VTW, 1988.

Villeneuve, Claude. *Tapisserie Dentelle: Pref. D'emmanuel Le Roy Ladurie.* Paris: Hachette, 1976.

Volbach, Wolfgang Fritz. *Early Decorative Textiles.* London: Hamlyn, 1969.

Wallace, L. (n.d.). *American Tapestry Alliance–ATA Linda Wallace Pages.* http://www.americantapestryalliance.org/AP/ArtistBio/WallaceL.html

Wallace, L. (2011). Blethering Crafts: *Linda Wallace.* Retrieved July 4, 2014, from http://bletheringcrafts.blogspot.ca/2011/05/linda-wallace.htm

Weibel, A. (1952) *Two thousand years of textiles: The figured textiles of Europe and the Near East.* New York: Pantheon Books.

Weigert, Roger-Armand. *French Tapestry.* London: Faber and Faber, 1962.

Wood Conroy, D. *An Archaeology of Tapestry: contexts, signs, and histories of contemporary practice.* Unpublished doctorate of creative arts thesis exegesis. Wollongong: University of Wollongong. 1995.

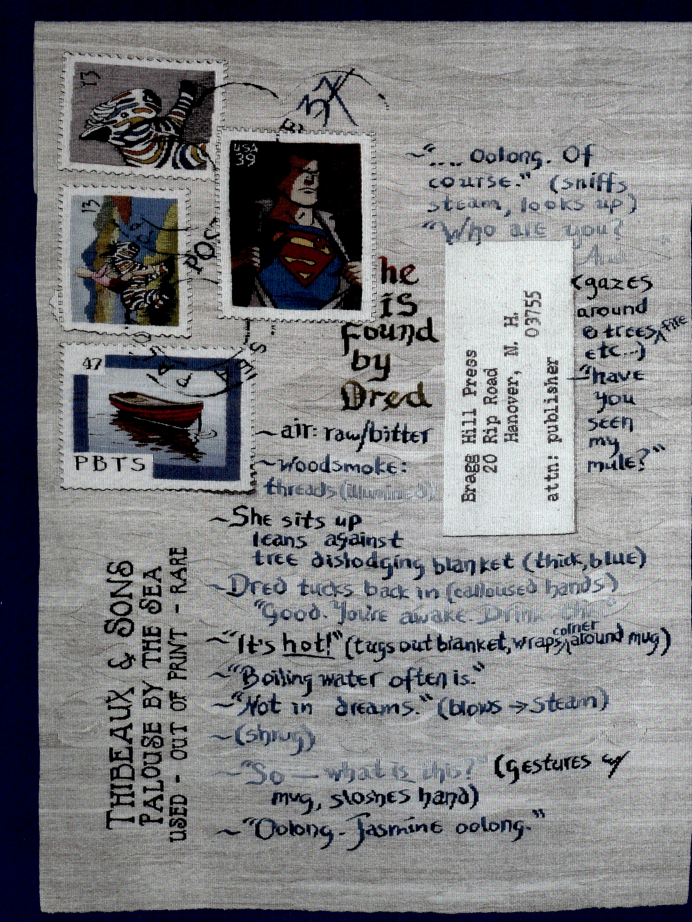

Appendix

Artists' Websites

Jo Barker: www.craftscotland.org/jobarker.html
Joan Baxter: www.joanbaxter.com
Helga Berry: www.fibercomposition.com
Rebecca Bluestone: http://rebeccabluestone.com
Archie Brennan: www.brennan-maffei.com
Elizabeth J. Buckley: http://ebuckleyartcampforadults.blogspot.com
Soyoo Park Caltabiano: http://www.soyooart.com
Wlodzimierz Cygan: www.cyganart.com
Alla Davydova: www.russianamericanculture.com/galleries/virtual-exhibitions/alla-davidova
Alexandra Friedman: www.alexfriedmantapestry.com
Ina Golub: http://www.inagolub.com
Barbara Heller: http://barbaraheller.ca
Susan Hart Henegar: http://www.susanharthenegar.com
Silvia Heyden: http://vimeo.com/25136243
Peter Horn: http://www.horn-tapestry-studio.homepage.t-online.de
Susan Iverson: http://susaniversonart.com/
Ruth Jones: http://www.ruthjones.ca
Aino Kajaniemi: http://www.elisanet.fi/aino.kajaniemi
Jane Kidd: http://www.janekidd.net
Christine Laffer: www.christinelaffer.com
Ewa Latkowska-Żychska: www.latkowska.pl/latkowska/eindex.html
Bojana H. Leznicki: www.bojanahleznicki.com
Susan Martin Maffei: http://www.brennan-maffei.com
Julia Mitchell: www.juliamitchelltapestry.com
Janet Moore: http://janetmooretapestry.com
Jon Eric Riis: http://www.jonericriis.com
Ramona Sakiestewa: www.ramonasakiestewa.com
Micala Sidore: http://www.hawleystreet.com
Elinor Steele: http://elinorsteele.com
Sarah Swett: www.sarah-swett.com

Galleries and Dealers

A.I.R. Gallery: www.airgallery.org
ACA Galleries: www.acagalleries.com
Bellas Artes Gallery: www.bellasartesgallery.com
Browngrotta Arts: www.browngrotta.com
Center for Book Arts (The): www.centerforbookarts.org
Cervini Haas Fine Art: www.cervinihaas.com
Chiaroscuro Contemporary Art: www.chiaroscurosantafe.com
Gail Martin Gallery: http://gailmartingallery.com
Gallery 51: www.gallery51.net
Konsthal Charlottenborg: www.kunsthalcharlottenborg.dk
Liljevalchs Konsthall: www.liljevalchs.stockholm.se
Melissa Morgan Fine Art: www.melissamorganfineart.com
Mobilia Gallery: www.mobilia-gallery.com
Noho Gallery: www.nohogallery.com
Robert Hillestad Textiles Gallery (The): http://textilegallery.unl.edu
Snyderman-Works Galleries: www.snyderman-works.com
Tyndall Gallery: www.tyndallgalleries.com
Tansey Contemporary: http://tanseycontemporary.com

Sarah C. Swett. *Rough Copy 7: Days Begin.* Handwoven tapestry: wool warp and weft, natural dye. 18 x 40" (45 x 100cm). Photo: Mark LaMoreaux.

"Palouse by the Sea," said Dred. "We start in the morning."

"Leave?" She clutched her pen, knuckles white. The nib bit into her palm.

"We're running out of food. I didn't pack enough for two and this is not the best season for foraging—as you may have noticed before the ~~mule~~ *isestimable* dumped your carcass by my fire."

"I'm sorry—"

Dred waved away the protest. "Got to get back sometime."

"To your...palace?"

"Pa-loose. It's a town. Half drowned and somewhat the worse for wear—so you'll fit right in." This with a smile.

"Then I should come?"

"Up to you." Dred shrugged. "It's a bit of a trudge. But I would be honored to have your company."

Hallmark STATION

Unearths needle and yarn mends socks — an anxious lattice of asparagus green

Museums and Collections

Albuquerque Museum of Art and History: www.cabq.gov/museum
American Textile History Museum: www.athm.org
Arizona State Museum–University of Arizona Gloria F. Ross Center for Tapestry Studies: http://www.tapestrycenter.org
Art Institute of Chicago: w.artic.edu/aic/collections/exhibitions/divineart/tapAIC
Asian Art Museum of San Francisco (The): www.asianart.org
Basl Historical Museum: http://www.hmb.ch/en/home
Bildmuseet: www.bildmuseet.umu.se
Brooklyn Museum of Art: www.brooklynmuseum.org
Burrell Collection: http://www.culturalpropertyadvice.gov.uk
Carnegie Museum of Art: http://web.cmoa.org
Centralne Muzeum Włókiennictwa (Central Museum of Textiles): www.muzeumwlokiennictwa.pl/muzeum
Château d'Angers: http://angers.monuments-nationaux.fr
Christiansborg Castle: http://www.christiansborg.dk/english
City Art Centre: http://www.edinburghmuseums.org.uk/Collections/Art-Collections/Fine-Art/Media/Tapestry
Clark Center for Japanese Art and Culture: http://www.ccjac.org
Cloisters (The): http://www.metmuseum.org
Cooper-Hewitt National Design Museum: www.cooperhewitt.org
Craft and Folk Art Museum: www.cafam.org
Cranbrook Art Museum: http://www.cranbrookart.edu/museum/CAMvu2.html
Denver Art Museum: www.denverartmuseum.org
Design Museum Designmuseo: www.designmuseum.fi
Dia:Beacon (Dia Art Foundation): http://www.diaart.org/sites/main/beacon
Dumbarton Oaks: http://www.doaks.org/museum/house
Fabric Workshop and Museum (The): www.fabricworkshop.org
Fine Arts Museums of San Francisco (The): http://www.famsf.org
Fuller Craft Museum: www.fullercraft.org
Fukuoka Art Museum: www.fukuoka-art-museum.jp
Galerie nationale de la tapisserie à Beauvais *and* **Manufacture nationale de Beauvais:** http://www.mobiliernational.culture.gouv.fr/en/practical-information/beauvais
Galerie des Gobelins *and* **Manufactures des Gobelins, de Beauvais et de la Savonnerie:** http://www.mobiliernational.culture.gouv.fr/en/practical-information/paris-gobelins
Gardner (Isabella Stewart) Museum: http://www.gardnermuseum.org/collection/artwork/2nd_floor/tapestryroom
Getty Museum (The J. Paul): http://www.getty.edu/art/
Guggenheim (Solomon R.) Museum: www.guggenheim.org
Hallwyl Museum (Hallwylska Museet): http://hwy.lsh.se
Hermitage Museum (The): http://www.hermitagemuseum.org
High Museum of Art: www.high.org
Hunterdon Art Museum: http://hunterdonartmuseum.org

Jewish Museum (The): http://www.thejewishmuseum.org
Kunsthistorisches Museum: http://ezine.codart.nl/17/issue/45/artikel/manifestations-of-habsburg-splendor--tapestries-in-the-kunsthistorisches-museum-vienna/?id=113
Lady Lever Art Gallery: http://www.liverpoolmuseums.org.uk/ladylever/collections/tapestries
LongHouse Reserve: www.longhouse.org
Los Angeles County Museum of Art: www.lacma.org
The Louvre: http://www.louvre.fr/en
MAD Museum of Arts and Design: http://collections.madmuseum.org
Mass MoCA: www.massmoca.org
McMullen Museum Boston College: http://www.bc.edu/bc_org/avp/cas/artmuseum/collections/index.html
Metropolitan Museum of Art (The): www.metmuseum.org
Minneapolis Institute of Arts: www.artsmia.org
Mississippi Valley Textile Museum: http://mvtm.ca/mvtm
MOMA Museum of Modern Art: http://www.moma.org
Musée des Arts décoratifs: www.lesartsdecoratifs.fr/english-439
Musée Jean Lurçat et tapisserie contemporaine: http://musees.angers.fr
Musée National du Moyen Âge, (The) formerly Musée de Cluny: http://www.musee-moyenage.fr
Musées Royaux d'Art et d'Histoire (Royal Art and History Museums): www.brusselsmuseums.be
Museum of Fine Arts, Boston: www.mfa.org
Museum of Indian Arts and Culture: http://www.indianartsandculture.org
Museum Victoria: http://museumvictoria.com.au/collections/themes/2617/australian-tapestry-workshop
National Museum of the American Indian (NMAI): www.nmai.si.edu

Sarah C. Swett. *Rough Copy 9: Red Paperclip*. Handwoven tapestry: wool warp and weft, natural dye. 52 x 28" (130 x 70cm). Photo: Mark LaMoreaux.

National Museum of Art, Architecture and Design (The): http://www.nasjonalmuseet.no/en
National Museum of Modern Art (The): www.momat.go.jp
National Museum of Women in the Arts: http://nmwa.org
Nederlands Textielmuseum: www.textielmuseum.nl
New Mexico Fiber Arts Trails: http://www.nmfiberarts.org
Newark Museum: http://www.newarkmuseum.org
Nordic Heritage Museum: www.nordicmuseum.org
Norton Simon Museum: http://www.nortonsimon.org/tapestries
Ölands Museum Himmelsberga: www.olandsmuseum.com
Philadelphia Museum of Art: http://www.philamuseum.org/collections/permanent/57731.html
Phillips Collection (The): http://www.phillipscollection.org
Princeton University Art Museum: www.princetonartmuseum.org
Prins Eugens Waldemarsudde: www.waldemarsudde.se
Renwick Gallery (The): http://americanart.si.edu
Röhsska Museum: http://rohsska.se/en/814
Royal Tapestry Factory: http://www.spain.info/en/que-qieres/arte/museos/madrid/real_fabrica_de_tapices.html
Rubin Museum of Art: http://www.rmanyc.org
SFMOMA (San Francisco Museum of Modern Art): www.sfmoma.org
San Jose Museum of Quilts & Textiles: http://www.sjquiltmuseum.org/collection.html
Sheldon Tapestry Maps of Warwickshire (The): http://heritage.warwickshire.gov.uk/museum-service/collections/the-sheldon-tapestry-maps
Spencer Museum of Art: http://www.spencerart.ku.edu/exhibitions/four-flemish-tapestries.shtml
Stedelijk Museum: www.stedelijk.nl
Suomen käsityön museo (The Finnish Craft Museum): www.craftmuseum.fi
Tapestry Museum Aix en Provence: http://en.aixenprovencetourism.com/aix-tapisserie-tipi.htm
Textile Center of Minnesota: http://www.textilecentermn.org
Textile Museum of Canada: www.textilemuseum.ca
Textile Museum (The): www.textilemuseum.org
Textile Museum (TextilMuseet): www.boras.se/textilmuseet
Timken Museum of Art: http://www.timkenmuseum.org/collection/french-tapestries
V&A Victoria and Albert Museum: http://www.vam.ac.uk/page/t/tapestry
Vatican Museums: http://mv.vatican.va
Wawel State Collections of Art: http://www.wawel.krakow.pl/en
Whitney Museum of American Art: www.whitney.org
Zimmerli Art Museum: http://www.zimmerlimuseum.rutgers.edu

Exhibitions

Arte&Arte. www.miniartextil.it
Biennale internationale di lin de Portneuf. http://www.biennaledulin.ca/
Fiberart International. http://fiberartinternational.org
International Triennial of Tapestry.
    www.muzeumwlokiennictwa.pl/aktualna-edycja/?lang=en
Kaunas Art Biennial. http://www.bienale.lt
From Lausanne to Beijing. www.chinafiberart.com.cn/
SOFA, Chicago, NYC, Santa Fe: www.sofaexpo.com
Snyderman-Works Galleries Biennial. http://www.snyderman-works.com/
    exhibitions/9th-international-fiber-biennial
Venice Biennale: http://www.labiennale.org/en/art/index.html

Sarah C. Swett. *Rough Copy 10: All Burned Up.* Handwoven tapestry: wool warp and weft, natural dye. 26 x 30" (65 x 75cm).
Photo: Mark LaMoreaux.

Periodicals

American Craft Magazine. www.americancraftmag.org
Art in America. www.artinamericamagazine.com
artforum.com. http://artforum.com
ARTnews. http://artnews.com
Circa Art Magazine. www.recirca.com
Craft Arts International Magazine (AU):. www.craftarts.com.au
Crafts Magazine - Crafts Council (UK).
    www.craftscouncil.org.uk/crafts-magazine
Gallery and Studio. www.galleryandstudiomagazine.com
Norwegian Crafts. www.norwegiancrafts.no
Selvedge. www.selvedge.org
Shuttle Spindle & Dyepot
    (Handweavers Guild of America). www.weavespindye.org
Surface Design Journal
    (Surface Design Association). www.surfacedesign.org
Taito (The Finnish Crafts Organization).
    www.taito.fi/en/taito-group/welcome
Textile: The Journal of Cloth and Culture.
    www.bergpublishers.com/BergJournals/Textile/tabid/518/Default.aspx
Textile Forum Magazine
    (European Textile Network). www.etn-net.org
Textilkunst. www.textilkunst.de
Vavmagasinet. www.vavmagasinet.se

Sarah C. Swett. *Rough Copy 11: Villa Algernon.* Handwoven tapestry: wool warp and weft, natural dye. 44 x 30" (110 x 75cm). Photo: Mark LaMoreaux.

Professional Organizations

American Tapestry Alliance (ATA). www.americantapestryalliance.org
British Tapestry Group (The). http://www.thebritishtapestrygroup.co.uk
Canadian Tapestry Network. www.canadiantapestrynetwork.com
Design & Crafts Council of Ireland. http://www.ccoi.ie
ETN—European Textile Network. http://www.etn-net.org/index.htm
Friends of Fiber Art International. http://www.friendsoffiberart.org
Gloria F. Ross Center for Tapestry Studies (The). http://tapestrycenter.org
Handweavers Guild of America. www.weavespindye.org
Moon Rain Centre for Textile Arts in the Outaouais.
   http://www.moonrain.ca/index.html
SDA Surface Design Association. http://www.surfacedesign.org
Tapestry Weavers West. http://tapestryweaverswest.org
TAPS—Tapestry Artists of Puget Sound. http://tapestryartists.org
Textile Center. http://www.textilecentermn.org
Textile Study Group of New York. http://www.tsgny.org
The Textile Society.
   http://www.textilesociety.org.uk/about-textile-society.php
TSA (Textile Society of America). http://textilesocietyofamerica.org/
WTA World Textile Art. http://www.wta-online.org

Sarah C. Swett. *Rough Copy 12: Do Not Bend.* Handwoven tapestry: wool warp and weft, natural dye. 98 x 23" (245 x 57.5cm).
Photo: Mark LaMoreaux.

Art Textiles Conservation and Restoration

The Cathedral of St. John the Divine:
The Textile Conservation Laboratory
  Marlene Eidelheit, Director
  1047 Amsterdam Ave. at 112th St.
  New York, NY 10025
  212-316-7523
  http://www.stjohndivine.org/about/textile-conservation-lab

Bojana Leznicki
  973-857-4602

Gail Martin Gallery
  310 Riverside Drive
  New York, NY 10025
  212-864-3550
  http://gailmartingallery.com

The mule picked her way down the
ghost of a road, skirting cellar holes
and rusting tractors. Dred sauntered
off to the side, pausing now and again
to pick a morel. Diana walked with her
eyes on the ground. Instead of mush-
rooms, she found a tiny doll peering
through a veil of bindweed.

"Sad," she murmured, unwrapping vines
from its belly.

"Hubris," said Dred.

"Oh?"

"These people thought the laws of
physics were for others, then fled
when the canyons began to fill.
They left us--" she beamed and
flung out her arms "--to this."

Diana lifted her head and
saw only mist, damp and grey,
then ripples,
then a splash
of color, a gusset
of land, a scrap
of possibility so enchanting
she recoiled. It was
a town like a child's toy
forgotten. Houses. People.
Decisions. Oh no. Not
yet. Not even if they had ink.
She wanted only this-- Dred and
Pearl, words without end, Amen.

But that night they camped on the
edge of the last trees. In the morning
they would be there.

Sarah C. Swett. *Rough Copy 13: There*. Handwoven tapestry: wool warp and weft, natural dye. 54 x 34" (135 x 85cm). Photo: Mark LaMoreaux.